Concepts of Object-Oriented Programming with Visual Basic

Springer
*New York
Berlin
Heidelberg
Barcelona
Budapest
Hong Kong
London
Milan
Paris
Santa Clara
Singapore
Tokyo*

Concepts of Object-Oriented Programming with Visual Basic

Steven Roman

With 24 Illustrations

 Springer

Steven Roman
Department of Mathematics
California State University
Fullerton, CA 92634
USA

Library of Congress Cataloging-in-Publication Data
Roman, Steven.
    Concepts of object-oriented programming with Visual Basic / Steven
Roman.
        p.   cm.
    Includes index.
    ISBN 0-387-94889-9 (softcover : alk. paper)
    1. Object-oriented programming (Computer science)   2. Microsoft
Visual BASIC.   I. Title.
QA76.64.R65   1997
005.265 — dc20   96-43296

Printed on acid-free paper.

Production managed by Victoria Evarretta; manufacturing supervised by Johanna Tschebull.
Camera-ready copy prepared from author's Microsoft Word files.
Printed and bound by R.R. Donnelley and Sons, Harrisonburg, VA.
Printed in the United States of America.

9 8 7 6 5 4 3 (Corrected third printing, 1998)

ISBN 0-387-94889-0 Springer-Verlag New York Berlin Heidelberg   SPIN 10669872

To Donna

Preface

This book is about object-oriented programming and how it is implemented in Microsoft Visual Basic. Accordingly, the book has two separate, but intertwined, goals. The first is to describe the general concepts of object orientation and the second is to describe how to do object-oriented programming in Visual Basic. I intend this to be a short, no-nonsense book that can be read through once and then easily referred to at later times. (Long stories about a mythical company and its programming problems are seldom interesting the first time through, let alone the second, third or fourth times!)

To read this book, you need only a *minimal* acquaintance with Visual Basic. In particular, I assume you can construct a simple Visual Basic program and have some rudimentary knowledge of fundamental programming techniques. This book does *not* teach Visual Basic — it teaches you how to program Visual Basic in an object-oriented way. The issue here is not how much Visual Basic you already know — it is that you want to learn about object-oriented programming techniques.

With regard to the first goal of the book, it is my feeling that a discussion of the underlying concepts of object orientation (just what *is* an *object*, a *class*, *encapsulation*, *abstraction*, and so on) is essential in order to take full advantage of any object-oriented language. Simply put, it will help you understand *what* you are doing if you know *why* you are doing it.

Let me put this issue in perspective with my own experience. I had been programming in earlier versions of Visual Basic for some time when I plunged into Visual Basic 4.0. As I usually do with a new application, or new version of an old application, I began by reading the documentation, turning to other books only when I felt that I needed some clarification — although this was seldom helpful. After spending a good deal of time poring over the manuals, I concluded that I could now follow the syntax and create an object-oriented program in Visual Basic. However, I was left with some very annoying questions, such as

- Why bother?
- What is the point of using object-oriented techniques?

- Yes, but what *is* an *object*, anyway?
- And what are these strange concepts like *abstraction* and *encapsulation*?

My only recourse for answering these questions was to dive into some more academic treatises on object orientation (which I *enjoy* doing). After consulting several books, I began to see some light. It felt as though a curtain had been raised, and I finally began to understand the *raison d'être* of object orientation — if not all of its subtleties.

I can't resist the temptation to share with you one example of the frustrations associated with trying to learn the basic issues of object orientation. Here is a quote from an excellent book (really) on the subject:

> The class **Class** is a subclass of the class **Object**; and thus, the object **Class** points to the object **Object** as its superclass. On the other hand, the object **Object** is an instance of the class **Class**; and thus, **Object** points back to **Class**. Class **Class** is itself a class, and thus an instance of itself.

To be entirely fair, this is not as confusing as it looks when taken out of context. But it does illustrate some of the difficulties in learning about object orientation. I wrote this book to help the reader get some insight into object-oriented programming without having to suffer through such frustrations.

I should also hasten to add, lest you think this book might be too academic, that this is definitely a book about Visual Basic. Thus, we will not dwell on abstract concepts in great depth, nor will we spend much time on aspects of object orientation that do not apply to Visual Basic.

The second goal of this book probably needs less motivation than the first, since I would guess that most people are more interested in *how* than in *why*. In any case, a concrete context helps clarify the abstract notions and provides a starting place for building object-oriented applications. As the title of the book suggests, we will use Visual Basic (version 4.0 or later) for this context.

Let me say a few words about my writing style: I will try to use only as many words as necessary in explaining the concepts and as few words as possible in dealing with the examples.

With regard to the examples, I find that I can learn much more quickly and easily by tinkering with and tracing through short program segments than by studying a long, detailed example. The difficulty in tinkering with a long program is that changing a few lines can affect other, perhaps irrelevant, portions of the code, to the point where the program will no longer run. Instead of wasting time trying to figure out *why* it will not run, I usually just give up.

On the other hand, if, for example, I want to experiment with how to break a circular reference in Visual Basic, I write a short program, of perhaps one or two dozen lines, with which to experiment. This is a great way to learn and also shows off the advantages of an interpreted language. I often save these little code snippets, for future tinkering. Accordingly, this book is filled with short code snippets. I encourage you to key them in and experiment with them yourselves.

Many books on object-oriented programming devote a great deal of space to program design issues, which are certainly important, especially for large projects involving lots of programmers. I shall leave this topic for others to write about.

The complete source code for the Turing Machine application (in Chapter 3) should be available on the Springer-Verlag Web site, under

http://www.springer-ny.com/supplements/sroman

Thanks for looking at my book. I hope you enjoy it.

Irvine, California   *Steven Roman*

Contents

Introduction

To understand the virtues of object-oriented programming, one needs to be aware of the context in which it is most useful. Some authors (I am not one) suggest that *all* Visual Basic programs be written using object-oriented techniques *exclusively*. But if a program is very small and will be coded by a single programmer, it may be easier to use a mixture of object-oriented techniques and non-object-oriented techniques. (I find that it seldom pays to be a snob about anything.)

On the other hand, the driving force in modern programming comes from two other areas. Many commercial programs, such as Microsoft Word, for example, are monumental efforts that take many programmers many months to code. This raises the issue of how one programmer's code interacts with another programmer's code, within the same application. Also, it is now possible, through OLE automation, for portions of one application's code to be made available to other applications. Again, this raises the issue of communication between code modules. (I use the term *code module* here in a generic sense, referring to a collection of code designed for a specific purpose. A code module may span many Visual Basic code modules.)

For reliable communication, a well-behaved code module should have certain properties. In a sense that we will make as precise as possible, a well-behaved code module should *encapsulate* its features into a nice, neat package that hides the details of the implementation and presents the user with a clearly defined and well-documented *public interface*. A well-behaved module should also include *data validation* wherever possible, with error messages to help the user quickly spot the source of problems.

As an example, consider a code module designed to compute information about a student's grade in a certain course (say Visual Basic 101). The code module might compute the student's average test score, median test score and letter grade, given his or her test scores for the course. A properly designed code module would take the input — in this case a series of test scores — and return the output, without troubling the user with the details of *how* the output was produced. This is encapsulation.

We can take this concept a step further by *abstracting* the notion of a student as follows. We define what is called an *abstract student class*. (Don't confuse the use of the term *class* with our use of the term *course*, such as Visual Basic 101, that a student might take. The term *class* has a specific meaning in object-oriented programming, and that is how we use it in this book.) This abstract student class is given *properties*, such as *StudentName, TestScore1, TestScore2* and *TestScore3*. We also define *procedures*, referred to as *methods* in object-oriented circles, for the class, such as *FindTheAverage, FindTheMedian* and *FindTheLetterGrade*. These procedures use the values of the *TestScore1, TestScore2* and *TestScore3* properties to compute their respective values, such as the average.

Each example, or *instance*, of the abstract student class represents an actual student. In object-oriented language, an instance is called an *object*. For example, suppose we want grade information about a particular student named Donna, who has test scores of 90, 85 and 100. We can then "request" that the student class "create" an instance of itself, that is, create an object of type student. We can then give that object the *StudentName* property *Donna* and set the test score properties, as follows:

```
StudentName = "Donna"
TestScore1 = 90
TestScore2 = 85
TestScore3 = 100
```

(This is not quite proper Visual Basic code, but it will serve to illustrate the point.)

We can then invoke the procedures of the abstract student class for the student object named Donna to get grade information about Donna. This is done using syntax such as

```
Donna.FindTheAverage
```

What we have done in this example is create an *abstract data type*, in this case a *student data type*. This process is referred to as *abstraction*, since we have abstracted *precisely* the properties and procedures of interest to us and removed all *irrelevant* information about students. In a sense, the student abstract data type is a "black box" (see Figure I.1) that acts like a student *only* in the sense that it has precisely the properties that we require (*StudentName, TestScore1, TestScore2, TestScore3*) and the procedures that we require (*FindTheAverage, FindTheMedian, FindTheLetterGrade*) with no extraneous stuff to get in our way. For instance, student objects do not have a height, weight or hair color property, because we don't need to define such properties for our purposes. On the other hand, real students certainly do have these properties (the hirsute ones, that is).

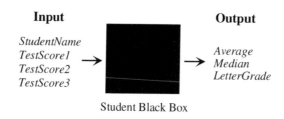

Figure I.1

One of the principal virtues of using abstract data types, such as the student data type, is that it permits code to be *reused*. For instance, the code in *FindTheAverage,* which is used to compute a student's average, is "built in" to the data type itself and thus the same code is used with all instances of that data type. For example, if we also create a student object with *StudentName* property *Steve*, we may obtain Steve's average by setting his *TestScore* properties and then running the *FindTheAverage* method:

```
StudentName = "Steve"
TestScore1 = 60
TestScore2 = 95
TestScore3 = 75
Steve.FindTheAverage
```

The last line will execute the *same code* as the line

```
Donna.FindTheAverage
```

but will use Steve's *TestScore* property values instead of Donna's.

The virtues of reusable code are fairly obvious. In particular, reusable code saves space and thereby improves performance. It also permits more robust coding, since changes to code (including bug fixes) are more easily and more accurately made when they only need to be made in one location. For instance, if we decide to take a weighted average of the test scores (say weighting the third score as half of the total grade), we would only need to make the necessary code changes within the data type itself, rather than have to make the same code change separately for each student.

The use of the same code in different situations is closely related to a concept known as *polymorphism* — a topic we will speak about briefly at the end of Chapter 1.

Another virtue of the abstract data type approach to programming can be described by the following example. Suppose we have, in our Visual Basic 101 course, some very gifted students. Of course, these students have the same properties and methods as all other students in the course, but we also want to consider some additional properties and methods for these students alone. For instance, we might want to consider the *StudentIQ* property of our gifted students. (It would be politically incorrect to consider IQs for nongifted students.)

Rather than start from scratch and define a new abstract data type, we can define a *subtype* of the student data type and include in the definition of this subtype only the *new* properties and methods. If we specify the new data type as a subtype of the student data type, it automatically *inherits* the properties and methods of the student data type. This procedure is referred to as *inheritance*. Its great virture is that it again permits code reusability since, for instance, we use the same code for computing averages for gifted students as for all other students.

Some would say that the implementation of *Encapsulation*, *Abstraction*, *Polymorphism* and *Inheritance* marks the sign of a true object-oriented programming language. As it happens, Visual Basic 4.0 supports the first three of these concepts but fails to support inheritance. Thus, you may hear it said that Visual Basic is not a true object-oriented language. This is really an unimportant issue. While there is no question that Visual Basic would be enhanced by an implementation of inheritance, it is still a very powerful language, with a unique position in the application programming world. It seems to me far more important to worry about how to take full advantage of the available power of the language, rather than waste time debating whether or not it fits into a certain pigeonhole.

Let me conclude this introduction with an apology. After making a point in the book to stress the importance of following certain object-oriented coding principles, I will be forced, in many examples, to ignore these very principles in order to save space and to focus more sharply on the issue at hand. Let me apologize for this now. The practice is intended only as an expediency, not as a recommendation.

Chapter 1
The Basics of Object-Oriented Programming

Data Types

We begin our discussion of object-oriented programming with a more familiar concept — that of a *data type*. What is a data type? For instance, what is the integer data type?

One possible answer is that, for Visual Basic, the integer data type is the set of integers from –32,768 to 32,767. However, this answer is not very stimulating and will not lead us to object-oriented ideas.

To provide a more fruitful answer, recall that all data are stored in a computer in *binary form*, as strings of 0's and 1's. Moreover, to a computer (that is, to the CPU), a binary string is just a string of 0's and 1's — no more and no less. The CPU knows how to push these strings around but does not attach a meaning or interpretation to them. It might be fair to say that the CPU recognizes only one data type, namely, the *bit* data type!

With this view in mind, we can say that the integer data type is a certain *way of interpreting* binary words — 16-bit binary words in the case of Visual Basic. Consider, for example, the 16-bit binary word 0100 0001 0100 0001. To the CPU, this is nothing more than a string of bits. To Visual Basic, it is also nothing more than that, until we give it an interpretation.

For instance, to tell Visual Basic to interpret this word as a string data type, we would write

```
Dim X as String
X = "AA"
```

since the ANSI code for "AA" is 0100 0001 0100 0001. To tell Visual Basic to interpret this word as an integer data type, we would write

```
Dim X as Integer
```

```
X = 16705
```

since the word in question is the binary representation of the integer 16705.

Now comes the key point. Interpreting a binary word as a particular data type (such as integer or string) implicitly gives that word certain *properties* and *operations*. For instance, a binary word of the integer data type has the *sign* property, which can take the values positive, negative or zero. In Visual Basic, the sign property is realized through the *Sgn* function, as in the following code:

```
Select Case Sgn(X)
Case 1
   MsgBox "Positive"
Case 0
   MsgBox "Zero"
Case -1
   MsgBox "Negative"
End Select
```

On the other hand, when the same binary word is interpreted as a string, it does not have the sign property. It does, however, have the *length* property, realized in Visual Basic by the *Len* function. Moreover, binary words of the integer data type have the usual arithmetic operations, such as negation, addition, subtraction and multiplication, whereas binary words of the string data type have the concatenation operation, for instance.

Since data types would not be of much use without their concomitant properties and operations, it makes sense to *define* a data type as a way of interpreting binary strings *together with* these properties and operations. Thus, the properties and operations are included as part of the *definition* of data type.

As we will see, this definition of data type has far-reaching consequences. It may seem at first that it makes no difference whether we include the properties and operations as part of the definition, or think of them as separate from the data type, as long as they are there. However, the purpose of including the properties and operations within the definition is more than cosmetic, since it allows for the *abstraction* of the concept of data type and signals the beginning of a new philosophy when thinking about coding issues. Part of this new philosophy is termed *encapsulation*.

Encapsulation

The idea of encapsulation is to contain (or "encapsulate") in one neat bundle the properties and behaviors (operations) that characterize an object. This serves three useful purposes:

- It permits the *protection* of these properties and behaviors from outside tampering by *exposing* only those portions that are needed in order to use the properties and behaviors.
- It allows the inclusion of *validation* code to help catch errors in the use of the exposed interface.
- It frees the user from having to know the details of how the properties and behaviors are implemented.

In a sense, all of learning involves encapsulation of concepts. Let us consider an example that involves the way computers store signed (that is, positive, zero and negative) integers and do arithmetic with these integers. Please bear with me, even if some of this seems a bit irrelevant at first — it will only take a couple of paragraphs.

As you undoubtedly know, an integer is stored in the memory of a PC as a string of 0's and 1's — called a *binary string*. This string needs to be interpreted in order to have meaning. In some languages, such as C, we may designate, for instance, that the string should be interpreted as a signed integer or as an unsigned integer, the difference being whether or not the number is allowed to be negative. This distinction is important because we have only limited space, and so, for instance, disallowing negative numbers gives us more room for nonnegative numbers.

In any case, Visual Basic does not provide us with this option. All integers are considered to be signed integers and are represented in the computer's memory in a form called *two's-complement representation*. The reason for the "fuss" is that there is no way to directly represent a negative sign in the computer's memory, and so a portion of the binary string itself must be used to represent the negative sign.

For simplicity, let us consider 8-bit binary numbers. An 8-bit binary number has the form $a_7a_6a_5a_4a_3a_2a_1a_0$, where each of the a_i's is a 0 or a 1. We can think of it as appearing in memory as shown below.

$$\boxed{a_7}\boxed{a_6}\boxed{a_5}\boxed{a_4}\boxed{a_3}\boxed{a_2}\boxed{a_1}\boxed{a_0}$$

As an example, consider the binary numbers

$$x = 11110000 \text{ and } y = 00001111$$

In the two's-complement representation, the leftmost bit a_7 (called the *most significant bit*) is the *sign bit*. If the sign bit is 1, the number is negative. If the sign bit is 0, the number is positive. Thus, x is negative and y is positive.

The formula for converting a two's-complement representation $a_7 a_6 a_5 a_4 a_3 a_2 a_1 a_0$ of a number to a decimal representation is

$$\text{decimal rep.} = -128a_7 + 64a_6 + 32a_5 + 16a_4 + 8a_3 + 4a_2 + 2a_1 + a_0$$

(note that the coefficients are just successive powers of 2). Thus, for instance, the decimal representation of the number x given above is

$$x = -128 + 64 + 32 + 16 = -16$$

and the decimal representation of y is

$$y = 8 + 4 + 2 + 1 = 15$$

To take the negative of a number when it is represented in two's-complement form, we must take the complement of each bit (that is, change each 0 to a 1 and each 1 to a 0) *and then add* 1. For instance, to form the negative of the number x, we first take the complement

$$00001111$$

which, in decimal form, is

$$8 + 4 + 2 + 1 = 15$$

and then we add 1, to get 16 (which is indeed the negative of -16).

Hopefully, at this point you are saying to yourself, "What is the point of this discussion? What does it have to do with object-oriented programming? I didn't buy this book to get a math lesson! As a programmer, I don't have to worry about these details. I just write code like

```
x = -16
y = -x
```

and let the computer and the programming language worry about which representation to use and how to perform the given operations."

If you are saying this, then you get the point! The details of how signed integers are interpreted by the computer (and the compiler) and how their properties and operations are implemented are *encapsulated* in the integer data type and are thus hidden from the user. Only those portions of the properties and operations that we need in order to work with integers are *exposed* outside of the data type. These portions form the *public interface* for the integer data type.

Moreover, encapsulation protects us from making errors. For instance, if we had to do our own negating by taking Boolean complements and adding 1, we might forget to add 1! The encapsulated data type takes care of this automatically.

Encapsulation has yet another important feature. Any code that is written using the public interface will remain valid even if the internal workings of the integer data type are changed for some reason, as long as the interface is not changed. For instance, if we move the code to a computer that stores integers in one's-complement representation, then the *internal* procedure for implementing the operation of negation in the integer data type will have to be changed, but from the programmer's point of view, nothing has changed. The code

```
x = -16
y = -x
```

is just as valid as before. What a relief.

Abstract Data Types

Encapsulation is so useful for data types that it makes sense to apply the concept to as many other objects as possible. Perhaps the best way to make this idea clear is through an example.

Consider a hypothetical teacher who wishes to write a program to keep students' exam grades for a particular course (say there will be three exams during the semester). Why not define an *abstract data type* named *Student* and give it some properties and operations?

The Student data type will have the properties *FullName*, *StudentID*, *Exam1*, *Exam2* and *Exam3*. The *FullName* and *StudentID* properties are strings and the *Exam1*, *Exam2* and *Exam3* properties are real numbers. The *Student* data type has two operations: *Average*, which returns a weighted average of the three exam grades (the third exam is the final), and *Pass*, which returns *yes* if the student passes the course or *no* if the student does not pass.

From now on, we will generally refer to operations as *methods*, because it is the term used in Visual Basic and it is better suited to abstract data types. While we are on the subject of terminology, in object-oriented programming circles, properties are also called *resources*, *attributes* or *member variables* and methods are also called *behaviors*, *services*, *operations*, *member functions* or *responsibilities* (yuck!).

An *abstract data type* is an *abstraction* of a basic (or shall we say concrete) data type, such as the integer data type. It has properties and operations, but it does not have quite the same concept of interpretation. To understand the differences between abstract and concrete data types, consider that the code

```
Dim X As Integer
X = 200
```

can be interpreted as follows:

> *Line 1*: Let X be a variable that refers to a 16-bit area of memory that will be *interpreted* as an integer. *Line 2*: Fill the area of memory referred to by X with the binary string 0000 0000 1100 1000, which is thus the binary representation of the integer 200.

For an abstract data type, we must be a little less "concrete." The code

```
Dim Donna As Student
Set Donna = New Student
```

can be interpreted as follows:

> *Line 1*: Let *Donna* be a variable that will refer to an abstract "object" of type Student (rather than to a memory location). *Line 2*: Create an object of that type and let *Donna* refer to that object.

From a programmer's perspective, the notion of a 16-bit area of memory is concrete — it is something we can visualize. On the other hand, the notion of an object doesn't bring anything concrete to mind. Instead, we may simply think of an object as a "black box" that Visual Basic manages in some arcane fashion. The concrete side of an object consists of its properties and methods, not where it is "located" in memory. In a sense then, an object is *defined* or *characterized* completely by its public interface!

From a practical point of view, since we seldom think about areas of memory when dealing with, say, an integer variable, there is little difference between a concrete and an abstract data type, although the latter tends to be more complex, in that it has many more properties and methods.

It is also interesting to note that abstract data types are built upon concrete data types. For instance, objects of the abstract *Student* data type have a *FullName* property, which takes as its value a member of the concrete *String* data type.

As we will see, properties of an object can also be of type *Object*, that is, an object can have a property whose value is another object. We will refer to such a property as an *object property*. For instance, an object of type *Student* can have a property of type *Teacher*. These objects in turn can have properties of type *Object*, and so on. Eventually, the chain of *object properties* must terminate in objects whose properties have concrete data types (such as integer or string).

The existence of object properties allows for the creation of *object hierarchies* in Visual Basic, an example of which is shown below. In this case, an object of type *Student* has three properties of type *Object* — *Advisor*, *Courses* and *Transcript*. The *Courses* object is a special type of object, known as a *collection object*. Collection objects are designed to hold other objects. This is important since, unless an object is either referred to by a variable or contained in a collection, it will be destroyed by Visual Basic.

The *Courses* collection object contains objects of type *Course*, that is, individual courses. Each object of type *Course* has an object property called *Professor*, which in turn has an object property called *Emolument*.

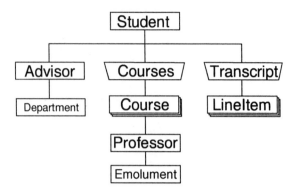

Object hierarchies can get quite complicated, but they have great advantages. For instance, they provide a *logical structure* to the program. We will discuss object hierarchies in more detail later in this chapter.

Classes

In many languages, including Visual Basic, abstract data types are implemented through *classes*. In general terms, a *class* is just a description of the properties and methods that define an abstract data type. In Visual Basic, a *class* is an actual code module that describes these properties and methods. Thus, a class is a *template* for making objects of a certain type. It is important not to confuse the template for building objects with the objects themselves. Put another way, it is important not to confuse the description of an object with the object itself.

Defining a Class in Visual Basic

To define a class in Visual Basic, we just insert a new class module and assign it a name in the *Properties* dialog box, for example, *CStudent*. Note that, as is customary, we prefix the letter "C" (for Class) to the class name.

If we want to think in a truly object-oriented manner, we should think of the class *CStudent* itself as a member of an abstract data type called *Class* (perhaps it should be *CClass*, but this is not customary). One of the properties of the class *Class* is *Name*. Simply put, every class has a name. The *Class* data type is managed by the Visual Basic IDE (integrated development environment) and has three properties: *Name*, *Instancing* and *Public*, as you can see from the *Properties* window of a class module, shown in Figure 1.1. (We will discuss the other two properties in the chapter on OLE automation.) When we use the *Insert Class* menu option in Visual Basic, we are actually creating a new object of type *Class*. Visual Basic then assigns to the object's *Name* property the default value *Class1* (or *Class2*, etc.).

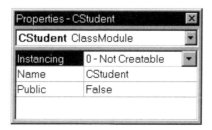

Figure 1.1

It is good programming practice to describe a newly created class in the *General Declarations* section of the class module. Thus, for the class *CStudent*, we might write

```
'' (In General Declarations Section)
' The Student Class CStudent
'
' Author: Steven Roman
' Date of last revision: Oct 1, 1066
'
' Properties:
' FullName
' StudentID
' Exam1, Exam2, Exam3
'
' Methods:
' Average
' Pass
```

(Code lines that begin with a double apostrophe are comments to the reader and are not intended to be included in the actual code. Thus, for instance, we will indicate the location of code by lines such as the first line of code above.)

Defining a Property in Visual Basic

In Visual Basic, a property is described by a *public* variable or by an *exposed* private variable (we will clarify this soon). Thus, we can make the following property declarations in the *General Declarations* section of the *CStudent* class module:

```
'' (In General Declarations Section)
' Properties
Public FullName as String
Public StudentID as String
Public Exam1 as Single
Public Exam2 as Single
Public Exam3 as Single
```

Defining a Method in Visual Basic

In Visual Basic, a method is just a *public* procedure (subroutine or function). Thus, the *Average* method for the *CStudent* class is defined as follows:

```
Public Function Average() as Single

' Exam scores must lie between 0 and 100
If Exam1 >=0 and Exam1 <= 100 and _
   Exam2 >=0 and Exam2 <= 100 and _
   Exam3 >=0 and Exam3 <= 100 then

   Average = 0.25*Exam1 + 0.25*Exam2 + 0.50*Exam3

Else

   '' Code here to display an error message

End If

End Function

Public Function Pass(pCutOff as Single) as Boolean

' Pass a student if average >= cutoff
If pCutOff <0 or pCutOff >100 then
```

```
'' Code here to display error message

Else

   If Average >= pCutOff then
      Pass = true
   Else
      Pass = False
   End If

End If

End Function
```

Exposing Properties Through the *Property Let*/*Set*/*Get* Procedures

There is one major problem with our implementation of the *CStudent* class —
it is *too public* and violates encapsulation principles. It is clear that methods
allow for the inclusion of validation code to "protect" them from untoward
usage. For instance, we have included validation code to prevent negative
exam scores and scores that exceed 100.

On the other hand, the value of a property set through a *public* variable can
be set from anywhere in the project and is not subject to validation. For
instance, student IDs may be required to be strings of length 10, but there is
nothing to prevent us, or someone coding another portion of the application,
from accidentally entering a *StudentID* of length 9. This might produce an
error down the road, when the property is used. However, at that point, it
might be very difficult to locate the offending code.

In order to prevent this, proper encapsulation dictates that we hide *direct
access* to the member variables, by declaring them *Private*. Then we expose
each property by means of two special methods — *Property Let* (or *Property
Set*, in the case of properties of type object) to set the property and *Property
Get* to retrieve the property. This will allow us to include validation code to
prevent the aforementioned peccadillo. Here is how the *StudentID* property
should be coded, for instance:

```
'' (In Declarations Section)
' Private member variable
```

```
Private mStudentID As String

Public Property Let StudentID(pID As string)

' Validate ID
If Len(pID) = 10 then
  mStudentID = pID
Else
  '' Code here to raise an error
End If

End Property

Public Property Get StudentID() As String

'' Getting the property requires no validation
StudentID = mStudentID

End Property
```

Note that the *private variable* holds the property, which is exposed through *public methods*. Thus, the public interface consists *entirely of methods*, which can contain validation code. This has the further advantage that we can easily make the *StudentID* property *read-only* by leaving out the *Property Let* method. In this case, the property can be set only through its private member variable, from *within* the class module. This would not be possible using property variables alone.

In the theory of object-oriented programming, the *Property Let* (and *Set*) method is referred to as an *update method*, since it updates the value of the property, and the *Property Get* method is referred to as an *accessor method*, since it accesses the value of a property. (Sometimes both property procedures are referred to as accessor methods.) These two methods are the key to encapsulation, since their presence implies that the public interface consists only of methods, which can perform validation.

As mentioned in the introduction to the book, for the sake of simplicity and to save space, we will reluctantly violate encapsulation principles in our examples, by often declaring properties using public variables.

Objects

A class is just a description of some properties and methods and does not have a life of its own. In fact, if we run a program that contains only an empty form, along with a class module filled with code, nothing much will happen — the code in the class module will not execute. To obtain something useful, we must create an *instance* of the class, officially known as an *object*. Creating an instance of a class is referred to as *instancing*, or *instantiating*, the class. (For some reason, one sometimes sees the inaccurate phrase *instance of an object*. The object *is* the instance.) We may create as many instances of a class as desired.

Instancing a class, that is, creating an object, is a two-step process in Visual Basic, because it is first necessary to declare a variable to use as a reference to the prospective object. Moreover, there are two forms of object creation — *explicit creation* and *implicit creation*.

Explicit Object Creation

To explicitly create an object of type *CStudent*, we use the code

```
Dim Donna As CStudent
Set Donna = New CStudent
```

The first line declares a variable named *Donna* to be of type *CStudent*. The second line asks Visual Basic to create an object of type *CStudent* and assign *Donna* as a *reference* to that object.

It is very important to keep a clear distinction between an object and a variable that refers to that object. It is the variable that we use in code. In fact, variables are the *only* means we have to use objects — we never really "see" the object itself.

To drive this point home, note that if we write

```
Dim Steve As CStudent
Set Steve = Donna
```

then *Steve* and *Donna* both point to (that is, refer to) the *same* object. Thus, we have two object variables but only one object.

The fact that object variables provide only *references* to objects can lead to confusion when many different object variables reference the same object. One area of potential problems arises when it comes time to destroy an object, since Visual Basic will not do so until *all* references to that object are removed. Thus, for instance, while the line

```
Set Donna = Nothing
```

removes the *Donna* reference to the object, the object is not destroyed, since *Steve* still holds a reference to that object.

Despite these facts, one often hears an expression such as "the object *Donna*" rather than "the object *referenced by Donna.*" Since the former usage is so common, we will feel free to use it as well, with the hope that no confusion will arise between a variable that points to an object and the object itself.

Instance Variables and Member Variables

There are some additional points that we should emphasize here. The line

```
Set Donna = New CStudent
```

not only creates an object, but assigns to that object *its own copy* of the member variables (both public and private) of the class *CStudent*. Simply put, each object gets its own copy of the member variables. These copies are referred to as the *instance variables* of the object. Thus, there is a distinction between member variables and instance variables. In a sense, member variables are never actually used as variables but serve as a "prototype" for the instance variables.

Thus, for example, if we write

```
Dim Bill as CStudent
Set Bill = New CStudent
```

then *Donna* and *Bill* will each have their own separate variables named *FullName*, *StudentID*, *Exam1*, *Exam2* and *Exam3*. To refer to *Donna*'s instance variables, the variable name must be *qualified*, as in

```
Donna.FullName
```

In fact, the expression *Donna.FullName* is called a *fully qualified property name.*

On the other hand, since *Donna* and *Steve* (from the previous subsection) point to the same object, they share that object's instance variables. Thus, the code

```
Steve.Exam1 = 20
```

implies also that *Donna.Exam1* equals 20. This is in contradistinction to the situation for ordinary variables, where, for example, if we execute the code

```
X = 5
Y = X
Y = 10
```

then the value of X is still 5.

Method names must also be qualified, to indicate which instance variables (if any) are to be used in the code for that method. Thus, to execute the *Average* method for *Donna*, we write

```
Donna.Average
```

The *Pass* method requires a parameter, as in

```
If Donna.Pass(65) then MsgBox "You Passed!"
```

It is important to emphasize that, while each instance of a class gets its own copy of the member variables, all instances share the same method code from the class. Thus, the lines

```
Donna.Average
```

and

```
Bill.Average
```

will cause the *same* lines of code to be executed. Of course, any references to member variables are replaced by the corresponding instance variables for the object in question. For example, when *Donna.Average* is executed, Visual Basic uses *Donna's* instance variables *Donna.Exam1*, *Donna.Exam2* and *Donna.Exam3*, whereas when *Bill.Average* is executed, Visual Basic uses *Bill's* instance variables *Bill.Exam1*, *Bill.Exam2* and *Bill.Exam3*.

Method code sharing is one of the most important advantages of object-oriented programming. In short, methods contain *reusable code*.

The *As Object* Syntax

If you have been programming with Visual Basic, then you may be familiar with the following syntax for declaring an object variable:

```
Dim Donna As Object
```

This line declares *Donna* as a variable of the generic abstract data type *Object* and thus allows *Donna* to reference *any* object. To illustrate, consider the following code:

```
' Declare Donna as a generic object variable
Dim Donna As Object

' Set Donna to reference a CStudent object
Set Donna = New CStudent
Donna.Name = "Donna Smith"
MsgBox Donna.Name

' Now set Donna to reference a Visual Basic form!
Set Donna = Forms.Item(0)
MsgBox Donna.Name
```

After setting the object variable *Donna* to point to a *CStudent* object, we then set the variable to point to a form object! (*Forms.Item(0)* refers to the first loaded form. We will discuss the *Forms* collection later in the chapter.)

It might seem that the use of generic object variables simplifies programming, since we don't have to decide ahead of time what type of object a given variable will reference. However, there is a performance penalty to pay for using generic object variables. We will say a few words about this issue now and postpone a thorough discussion until the chapter on OLE automation, where the issue is most keenly felt.

Visual Basic can determine the type of object that is referenced by a variable (also known as *resolving a variable reference* or *binding a variable*) either at compile time or at run time. Resolving references at compile time produces a more efficient executable file, since the file does not need to contain the extra code needed to do the referencing.

When we use specific object types rather than generic object types, such as *CStudent* instead of *Object*, or *Textbox* instead of *Control*, or *Integer* instead of *Variant*, Visual Basic can bind the variables at compile time, which is more desirable. This is particularly important when there are lots of object variables, or when using OLE automation objects, as we will see in a later chapter. The moral is: For improved performance, be as specific as possible when declaring variables.

Implicit Object Creation

As we have seen, the second line in the following code

```
Dim Donna As CStudent
Set Donna = New CStudent
```

asks Visual Basic to create an object of type *CStudent* and assign *Donna* as a reference to that object. Visual Basic provides an interesting and often useful alternative to this *explicit* object creation, which we will refer to as *implicit object creation*.

Implicit object creation is done by replacing the two lines above with the following single line:

```
Dim Donna as New CStudent
```

The effect of this line is to declare *Donna* as a variable of type *CStudent*, but it does not *immediately* create an instance of the *CStudent* class. However, Visual Basic will create an instance of *CStudent* and point *Donna* to that instance the first time the variable *Donna* is used. For example, the line

```
Donna.FullName = "Donna Smith"
```

will cause Visual Basic to create a *CStudent* object (that is, assuming this is the first line in which the variable *Donna* is used).

We will see examples of the use of both explicit and implicit object creation when we discuss object properties a bit later in this chapter.

It is probably true that explicit object creation is the better programming practice, since we have precise control over when objects are created. Under implicit object creation, the point at which an object is created depends upon when it is first referenced. Thus, we might add a seemingly innocuous new line of code to a program that was written many months earlier, and thereby unwittingly change the point at which an object is created. Generally, this is not a problem. However, as we will see, when an object is first created, Visual Basic fires a special event called the *Initialize event* for that object. If we have placed some time-sensitive code in that event, a change in the creation time of an object could potentially cause problems.

On the other hand, we will see in the chapter on OLE automation that there are circumstances that require the use of implicit object creation. Thus, a good general working rule is to use explicit object creation (even though it takes a few extra lines of code) unless implicit object creation is required.

Referencing Public Variables and Procedures

For the sake of reference, let us pause to collect in one place the rules for declaring and referencing *Public* variables and procedures in Visual Basic. Note that the rules depend on the type of module in which the variable or procedure is defined.

- Public variables and procedures can be defined in the *General Declarations* section of a module only — not within procedures.
- Public variables and procedures can be defined in any type of module (form, standard or class).
- A public variable or procedure defined in a standard module can be used throughout the project without qualification.
- A public variable or procedure defined in a form module must be *qualified* with the form name before it can be addressed. For example, if a form module named *frmMain* has a public variable or procedure named *Pub*, then the proper syntax for accessing this variable or procedure from other parts of the project is *frmMain.Pub*.
- A public variable or procedure defined in a class module must be *qualified* before it can be addressed. However, unlike the case for form modules, if a class named *TestClass* has a public variable or procedure named *Pub*, then we *cannot* address this variable or procedure as *TestClass.Pub*, for the simple reason that *TestClass* is not an object; it is a class (or *template* for an object). To qualify a public variable or procedure from a class module, you must first instance that class and then use the instance name as a qualifier, as in

```
Dim ctest As New TestClass
```

```
Call ctest.Pub
```

- You cannot define a public fixed-length string or array (or constant or Declare) in a Form or Class Module.

Note that procedures and properties in different modules can have the same name. As long as the fully qualified names are different, there is no problem accessing the correct procedure or property. Some authors suggest that you should not use the same name in different modules, because it can cause confusion. However, this advice precludes taking advantage of an important programming technique known as *overloading*. In fact, Visual Basic does this very thing all the time, as in, for example, *frmMain.ScaleHeight* and *frmOther.ScaleHeight*.

The Object/Message Model

Let us take a moment to describe a slightly different way of thinking about an object's methods. This is strictly a *Gedanken experiment* (that is, a thought experiment), since it does not have any *practical* significance for Visual Basic programmers. Nonetheless, it is an extremely important view for Windows programmers.

Consider again the *CStudent* class and its *Average* method. If we create an instance of this class, say

```
Dim Donna as CStudent
Set Donna = New CStudent
```

then we would interpret the code

```
Donna.Average
```

as a call to *Donna's* version of the procedure *Average*. (By *Donna's version*, we mean the *Average* procedure that uses *Donna's* instance variables.) Thinking of objects as "owning" procedures that can be called from other objects (or locations) might be termed the *procedure-oriented model* of object-oriented programming.

However, it is common in object-oriented circles to take a somewhat different view of the communication between objects. Namely, we can think of an object as able to respond to *messages* from other objects. Under this model, the code

```
Donna.Average
```

sends the *Average message* to the object referenced by *Donna*. This object is called the *target object* of the message. Similarly, the code

```
Bill.Average
```

sends the *Average* message to the target object referred to by the variable *Bill*.

In this model, the methods of the class *CStudent* are the messages to which a target object of type *CStudent* can respond. This set of messages is referred to in object-oriented terminology as the *protocol* of the class. The message paradigm is heavily used in Windows programming, but not used directly in Visual Basic programming.

The *Me* Keyword

It is interesting to observe that often there is no *direct* reference in the code of a class module to the target object. This is the case for the code in the *CStudent* class module, for instance. Of course, the target object may be referred to *indirectly* through its instance variables, as in the method *Average*, but even this is not necessary.

On the other hand, there may be times when we want to make an explicit reference to the target object. This is done in Visual Basic using the *Me* keyword. Here is a simple example.

Snippet 1.1

In a new project, insert a class module and include the following code. The method *IncWeight* uses the keyword *Me* to refer to the target object.

```
'' (Class module Class1)
Public MyWeight As Integer

Public Sub Add1()
MyWeight = MyWeight + 1
End Sub
```

```
' Public method using Me keyword
Public Sub IncWeight()

' Invoke the Add1 method for the target object
' using self-reference
Me.Add1

' Refer to MyWeight property of the target object.
MsgBox "If my weight was one greater, it would be "
& Me.MyWeight

End Sub
```

In the *Form_Load* procedure of the form module, place the following code:

```
Private Sub Form_Load()

' Implicit creation of object
Dim Steve As New Class1

' Set the property
Steve.MyWeight = 130

' Run the method that uses the Me keyword,
' which will refer to the target object Steve
Steve.IncWeight

End Sub
```

Running the project will result in the message

```
If my weight was one greater, it would be 151
```

Object Properties and Object Hierarchies

We have seen examples of *String* properties; that is, properties that have the *String* data type (such as *FullName*). We have also seen examples of *Single* properties, which are properties that have the *Single* data type (such as *Exam1*).

A property can have any ordinary data type *except* fixed-length string or array. (However, we can easily get around the restriction on array variables by storing the array in a variable of type *Variant*, which is a property type. This is done in the Turing machine example presented in a later chapter.)

As mentioned earlier, a property can also have an abstract data type, that is, a property of one class can take, as its value, an object of another class. We will refer to such a property as an *object property*.

The following code snippet illustrates the use of object properties. Note that we will have several occasions throughout this chapter to enhance this code to illustrate other concepts. For this reason, we suggest that you key in the code on your own system, so that you can make the modifications yourself as we continue.

Snippet 1.2 — The CStudent Class

In a new project, create a class module called *CReportCard* and add the following code:

```
'' (In Class CReportCard)
Public MathGrade As String
Public EnglishGrade As String
```

In a new class module named *CStudent*, add the following code, which defines an object property of type *CReportCard*. Note that we have exposed the property through the *Property Let/Property Set* methods.

```
'' (In Class CStudent)
' A property of CStudent that is of type CReportCard
Private mReportCard As CReportCard

Public Property Get ReportCard() As CReportCard
Set ReportCard = mReportCard
End Property

Public Property Set ReportCard(pReportCard As
CReportCard)
Set mReportCard = pReportCard
End Property
```

Finally, in the *Form_Load* event of the form module, add the following code and then save the project.

```
Private Sub Form_Load()

' Create object of type CStudent
Dim objStudent As CStudent
Set objStudent = New CStudent

' Create object of type CReportCard
' (using explicit object creation)
Dim objReportCard As CReportCard
Set objReportCard = New CReportCard

' Set the ReportCard property of the former
' object to the latter object
Set objStudent.ReportCard = objReportCard

' Set the object property's properties
objStudent.ReportCard.MathGrade = "A"
objStudent.ReportCard.EnglishGrade = "B"

' and show them
MsgBox "Math Grade: " &
objStudent.ReportCard.MathGrade

MsgBox "English Grade: " &
objStudent.ReportCard.EnglishGrade

End Sub
```

When an *instance variable* of one object holds a reference to another object, we say that the first *object* holds a reference to the second object.

The previous code snippet creates the beginnings of an *object hierarchy*, which is created when objects of one class (the *parent class*) hold references to objects of another class (the *child class*). In the example above, the parent class is *CStudent* and the child class is *CReportCard*, as indicated by the following figure.

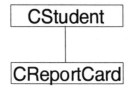

Object hierarchies provide some very useful benefits. For instance, they allow the programmer to create a logical (parent/child) structure for the objects in a project. Microsoft refers to this as a *containment* relationship — parent objects *contain* child objects — a terminology that no doubt comes from the examples of form objects containing control objects, as child objects. This logical organization can be a big help in a highly complex program, with dozens of classes, many of which are related to other classes. We will encounter a more elaborate object hierarchy when we consider a complete example of object-oriented programming in the chapter on the Turing Machine.

Explicit Creation Versus Implicit Creation

The code in Snippet 1.2 employs *explicit* object creation for the *ReportCard* property, in the lines

```
Dim objReportCard As CReportCard
Set objReportCard = New CReportCard
```

The *ReportCard* property was then set to refer to this object with the line

```
Set objStudent.ReportCard = objReportCard
```

An alternative is to use *implicit* object creation. First, we change the property declaration

```
Private ReportCard As CReportCard
```

in the *CStudent* class to

```
Private ReportCard As New CReportCard
```

(note the *New* keyword). We can then remove the code that explicitly creates the *CReportCard* object from the *Form_Load* event, reducing it to the following snippet.

Snippet 1.3 — The CStudent Class (Implicit Creation)

```
Private Sub Form_Load()

' Create object of type CStudent
Dim objStudent As CStudent
Set objStudent = New CStudent

' Implicitly create object of type CReportCard
' and set object properties
objStudent.ReportCard.MathGrade = "A"
objStudent.ReportCard.EnglishGrade = "B"

' and show them
MsgBox "Math Grade: " &
objStudent.ReportCard.MathGrade

MsgBox "English Grade: " &
objStudent.ReportCard.EnglishGrade

End Sub
```

If you make the above changes yourself and trace through the code, you will see that the line

```
objStudent.ReportCard.MathGrade = "A"
```

causes execution to switch to the *Property Get ReportCard()* procedure in the *CStudent* class:

```
Public Property Get ReportCard() As CReportCard
Set ReportCard = mReportCard
End Property
```

The *Set* line in this procedure is the first use of the *mReportCard* object variable referred to in the implicit declaration

```
Private ReportCard As New CReportCard
```

and thus triggers the implicit creation of the *CReportCard* object.

The two approaches (explicit versus implicit object creation) are illustrated in Figure 1.2.

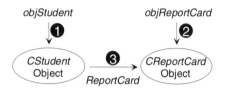

(a) Explicit creation

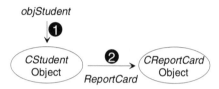

(b) - Implicit creation

Figure 1.2

We can describe these two approaches as follows:

Explicit creation (The child property has been declared in parent class.):
- Explicitly create the parent object of type *CStudent*.
- Explicitly declare a variable and create an object of the child type *CReportCard*.
- Form the parent/child link, through the property value, with the line

```
Set objStudent.ReportCard = objReportCard
```

Implicit creation (The child property has been declared in parent class, using the *New* keyword.):
- Explicitly create the parent object of type *CStudent*.
- *Use* the child property, as in

```
objStudent.ReportCard.MathGrade = "A"
```

which will automatically create a child object and form the parent/child link.

The main difference between these two approaches is that the former gives more control over *when* the *CReportCard* object is created and also provides an independent reference to that object, through the variable *objReportCard*. This can be useful in dealing with object destruction and circular references (see below), but if it is not needed, then the implicit approach makes more efficient use of resources, since it does not create a superfluous object variable.

Although in the situation above we may use either explicit or implicit object creation, we will see when we discuss object collections and again in the chapter on OLE automation that there are situations where implicit object creation is the best (or perhaps the only) way to achieve certain goals. For instance, we may want another application to use our *CStudent*/*CReportCard* object hierarchy, but we may not to be able to create a *CReportCard* object without first creating a *CStudent* object that owns the report card. This goal can be achieved only by permitting the creation of a *CReportCard* object indirectly, by *referring* to the *CReportCard* property of an existing *CStudent* object. This reference causes Visual Basic to implicitly create the desired *CReportCard* object. We will discuss this further in the chapter on OLE automation.

Creating and Destroying Objects

In a true objectcentric environment, everything is an object, that is, an instance of a class. As we have already discussed, in Visual Basic, a class is also an object — an instance of an abstract data type called *Class*. Instancing the *Class* data type (that is, creating a class module) is done by selecting the *Class Module* menu choice from the *Insert* menu in Visual Basic.

Since class modules are instances of the *Class* data type, they have the properties and methods of that data type. In particular, the properties of an object of type *Class* are *Name*, *Instancing* and *Public* and are shown in the *Properties* window of the Visual Basic IDE.

Visual Basic provides the *Class* data type with two rather special methods that act on its instances, that is, on class modules. One method creates objects of the class and the other destroys objects of the class. These methods are special because we don't access them in the usual way. In fact, we can't access the method for destroying objects at all!

Creating Objects

You might think at first that the syntax for creating an object should be something like

```
Set Donna = CStudent.CreateObject
```

or

```
Set Donna = CreateObject("CStudent")
```

But, as we have already seen, the syntax is

```
Set Donna = New CStudent
```

(Actually, as we will see in a later chapter, the penultimate syntax is used to create an OLE automation object.)

The work done by Visual Basic in creating objects is transparent to the programmer. However, we do have an opportunity to add to that work. Whenever an object is created, a special event called the *Initialize event* is fired for that object. Of course, the purpose of this event is to allow initialization code for objects of the given type. For instance, we may want to set some of the object's properties in this event, or we may simply want to alert the user, via a *MsgBox,* that an object has been created. (The *Initialize* event is also a useful debugging tool, since it enables the programmer to determine precisely when an object is created.) To see the *Initialize* event in action, try the following.

Snippet 1.4

In a new project, create a class module and insert a property.

```
Public TestProp as String
```

Then, in the *Initialize* event of this class, place the code

```
Private Sub Class_Initialize()
MsgBox "Class1 object initializing."
End Sub
```

Finally, to the *Form_Load* event, add the code

```
Private Sub Form_Load()
Dim objTest as Class1
Set objTest = New Class1
End Sub
```

Trace through this project and watch the code execute. Execution should switch to the *Initialize* event after executing the final line of code in the *Form_Load* event.

Note that the *Initialize* event fires immediately *after* the creation of an object, so the programmer has access to all of the object's properties and methods.

Destroying Objects

Some programming languages (such as Pascal and C++) provide an explicit command to destroy an object, but Visual Basic does not. By providing an explicit destruction command, the programmer has complete control over the life of an object. However, for this very reason, he or she can destroy that object even if it still has outstanding references, which then become *dangling references*. It can be very tiresome to have a piece of code destroy an object while you are in the middle of using a variable that references that object!

Visual Basic handles the destruction of objects *implicitly*. In particular, an object is destroyed automatically when there are no longer any references to that object; that is, when *all* variables that reference the object have gone either out of scope or have been set to *Nothing*, as in

```
Set Donna = Nothing
```

Let us look at some sample code to demonstrate the destruction of objects by Visual Basic. In this example, we place code in the *Terminate event* of a class module. This event is fired just prior to the destruction of an object. (Incidentally, once the *Terminate* event has begun, there is no way to stop the destruction of the object. There is no *cancel* parameter, as there is in the *Unload* and *QueryUnload* events.)

Snippet 1.5

In a new project, create a class and place the following code in the *Terminate* event:

```
Private Sub Class_Terminate()
MsgBox "Class1 object terminating."
End Sub
```

Then place a text box named *Text1* on the main form and add the following code to the *Form_Load* event.

```
Private Sub Form_Load()

Dim objTest1 As Class1
Dim objTest2 As Class1

Set objTest1 = New Class1
Set objTest2 = New Class1

' Fires terminate event for objTest2
Set objTest2 = Nothing

' When textbox gets focus, objTest1 goes out
' of scope and terminate event fires
Show
Text1.SetFocus

End Sub
```

In tracing through the code above, notice that the *Terminate* event fires in response to the removal of the reference *objText2* (by setting it to *Nothing*) and fires again when *Text1* gets the focus, since at that time the variable *objTest2* goes out of scope, releasing the reference to its object.

Also try tracing through the following code in the *Form_Load* event. This code emphasizes the point that an object is not destroyed until *all* of the references to it have been removed.

```
Private Sub Form_Load()
```

```
Dim objTest1 As Class1
Dim objTest2 As Class1

Set objTest1 = New Class1

' Create a second reference to the same object
Set objTest2 = objTest1

' Does not fire terminate event
Set objTest = Nothing

' Fires terminate event
Set objTest2 = Nothing

End Sub
```

Reference Counts

Garbage collection is a colorful term referring to the reclamation of the resources used by objects that are no longer needed (in short, destroying objects). Visual Basic implements garbage collection by keeping a *reference count* on each object in a running application. This count is simply the number of variables that reference the object. Note that the reference count is *not* necessarily equal to the number of other objects that reference the object — since one object can reference another object through more than one instance variable.

When a reference to an object is created, the object's reference count is incremented by one. When a reference is removed, the reference count is decremented by one. When an object's reference count reaches zero, the object is destroyed by Visual Basic.

One of the benefits of the reference count approach is that it prevents the problem of dangling references. On the other hand, the reference count approach may require a considerable amount of overhead on the part of Visual Basic, in order to keep track of the reference counts for hundreds or perhaps thousands of objects in a given application. Consider that, when the reference count of one object reaches zero, the object is destroyed. But if that object is referenced by other objects, then their reference counts must also be adjusted, which might cause other objects to be destroyed. This could cause a chain reaction that might take considerable time and resources to resolve.

Circular References

Implicit destruction of objects brings with it some potential headaches, chief among which is *circular references*, which happens when one object holds a reference to another object, which in turn holds a reference (directly or indirectly) to the first object. While this is happening, Visual Basic cannot destroy either object.

To get a clear picture of what happens with circular references, we will consider three examples, beginning with the simplest possible form of circular reference — an object that refers directly to itself.

Snippet 1.6 — The CStudent Class: Direct Self-Reference

In the *CStudent* class, add the following property, of type *CStudent*:

```
Public SelfRef as CStudent
```

In the *Terminate* event for *CStudent*, place the code

```
Private Sub Class_Terminate()
MsgBox "CStudent object terminating."
End Sub
```

The *Form_Load* event should contain the following code. (You should delete or comment out any remaining code from previous examples.)

```
Private Sub Form_Load()

' Create object of type CStudent
Dim objStudent As CStudent
Set objStudent = New CStudent

' Set it to refer directly to itself
Set objStudent.SelfRef = objStudent
```

```
Set objStudent = Nothing

End Sub
```

The situation created by the code above is pictured in Figure 1.3.

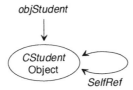

Figure 1.3

Note that the reference count for the *CStudent* object is 2, since *objStudent* and *SelfRef* both point to that object.

Note also that running the code in the *Form_Load* event does *not* cause the *Terminate* event for the *CStudent* class to fire, since releasing the *objStudent* reference does not release *all* references to the object. In fact, the object is still alive because its *own* instance variable, *SelfRef*, holds a reference to the object.

Now we are in some trouble, since this "internal" variable is the *only* reference to the object, and since we have lost the only access that we had to the variable, which was through *objStudent.SelfRef*. As long as the application is running, the *CStudent* object will remain alive and use resources.

Our only chance to remove the self-reference was *before* we removed the external reference *objStudent*. Thus, had we placed the line

```
Set objStudent.SelfRef = Nothing
```

before the last line above, then the *Terminate* event would have fired when the *objStudent* reference was removed.

The next example does not involve a circular reference, but we need it for contrast with the example following it.

Snippet 1.7 — The CStudent Class: No Self-Reference

The line

```
Public ReportCard as CReportCard
```

should already be present in the *CStudent* class. If not, then add it now. In the *Terminate* event for *CReportCard*, place the code

```
Private Sub Class_Terminate()
MsgBox "CReportCard object terminating."
End Sub
```

(You should still have analogous code in the *Terminate* event for the *CStudent* class.)

The *Form_Load* event should contain the following code. (Again, you should delete or comment out any other code from previous examples.)

```
Private Sub Form_Load()

' Create object of type CStudent
Dim objStudent As CStudent
Set objStudent = New CStudent

' Create object of type CReportCard
Dim objReportCard As CReportCard
Set objReportCard = New CReportCard

' Set the WhichStudent property of objReportCard
' to refer to objStudent
Set objReportCard.WhichStudent = objStudent

Set objStudent = Nothing
Set objReportCard = Nothing

End Sub
```

Figure 1.4 illustrates the above code.

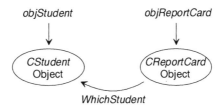

Figure 1.4

When the line

```
Set objStudent = Nothing
```

is executed, the reference count for the *CStudent* object is reduced to 1. When the line

```
Set objReportCard = Nothing
```

is executed, the reference count for the *CReportCard* object is reduced to 0, thus causing Visual Basic to destroy the object. This causes the *WhichStudent* instance variable to go out of scope, further reducing the reference count for the *CStudent* object to 0, causing it to be destroyed as well. This is why both *Terminate* events will fire, as you can see if you trace through the code.

Now we are ready for the third example.

Snippet 1.8 — The CStudent Class: Indirect Self-Reference

In the *CStudent* class, place the code

```
' Property of type CReportCard
Public ReportCard As CReportCard

Private Sub Class_Terminate()
MsgBox "CStudent terminate event fired."
End Sub
```

In the child class *CReportCard*, put

```
' Property of type CStudent
Public WhichStudent As CStudent
```

```
Private Sub Class_Terminate()
MsgBox "CReportCard terminate event fired."
End Sub
```

The *Form_Load* event should contain the following code:

```
Private Sub Form_Load()

' Create an object of type CStudent
Dim objStudent As CStudent
Set objStudent = New CStudent

' Create an object of type CReportCard
Dim objReportCard As CReportCard
Set objReportCard = New CReportCard

' Set the ReportCard property of the former object
' to the latter object
Set objStudent.ReportCard = objReportCard

' Now make a circular reference
Set objStudent.ReportCard.WhichStudent = objStudent
'' (Or equivalently,
''    objReportCard.WhichStudent = objStudent)

' Remove reference to CStudent object
Set objStudent = Nothing

' Remove reference to CReportCard object
Set objReportCard = Nothing

End Sub
```

The picture for this code is in Figure 1.5.

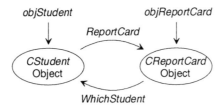

Figure 1.5

Running this code also fails to fire any *Terminate* events. To understand why, let us look at the reference counts. Figure 1.5 shows that the reference count for each object is 2. In fact, the *CStudent* object references the *CReportCard* object, through the instance variable *ReportCard*, and the *CReportCard* object references the *CStudent* object, through the instance variable *WhichStudent*. This accounts for the circular reference. In addition, each object is referenced by the object variable used to create the object. This is why each object has two references.

Now, the line

```
Set objStudent = Nothing
```

frees one reference to the *CStudent* object, but does not cause the object to be destroyed. Hence, the instance variable *ReportCard* still refers to the *CReportCard* object. The line

```
Set objReportCard = Nothing
```

frees one reference to the *CReportCard* object but since the *ReportCard* variable still holds a reference to this object, it is not destroyed. We now have the situation pictured in Figure 1.6, where we no longer have access to either of the instance variable references. Accordingly, the two objects will remain in memory until the application terminates.

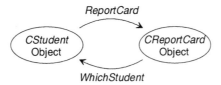

Figure 1.6

To properly clean up, we should have removed at least one of the instance variable references first. For example, adding the line

```
Set objStudent.ReportCard = Nothing
```

before the line

```
Set objStudent = Nothing
```

would do the trick. Give it a try.

The moral of these examples is that an object may be referenced by two different types of variables. An *external* reference is through a variable that is *not* an instance variable of any class (including the class that created the object). An example is the *objStudent* variable. An *internal* reference is a reference made through an instance variable of some object. An example is the *ReportCard* variable. To break an internal reference, we must use an external variable. Hence, if the *only* references to the objects in a circular reference are internal references (as in Figure 1.6), then we have no access to the circle and hence no way to "break" the circle.

The Notorious *End* Statement

Let us make one more important point about object destruction. Referring to Snippet 1.8, if we run this program, the end result will be a blank form. Closing the form using Alt-F4 will cause the *Terminate* events to fire for both objects.

Also, if we put the statement

```
Unload Me
```

at the end of the existing code in the *Form_Load* event, the *Terminate* events will fire. However, if we instead put an *End* statement at the end of this code, the application will close but the *Terminate* events will *not* fire!

The lesson here is that, as the Visual Basic documentation states:

> Understand that the *End* statement stops execution abruptly, without invoking the *Unload*, *QueryUnload*, or *Terminate* event . . . . For normal termination of a Visual Basic program, it is recommended that you unload all forms.

How to Control a Circular Reference — A Linked List Example

We don't want to leave the impression that circular references are necessarily bad — they just require some circumspection. In fact, there are times when circular references are very useful, and so it can be important to develop techniques for handling such references. This subsection describes one such example. It can be skipped on the first reading of the book, if desired.

You may be familiar with the concept of a *doubly linked list*, which is a structure used to store data. A small (three-item) doubly linked list is pictured in Figure 1.7.

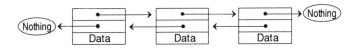

Figure 1.7

Each item in the list has three parts: One part contains a reference to the next item in the list; one part contains a reference to the previous item in the list; and one part holds the data. A doubly linked list is a very efficient way to store data that need to be traversed quickly. Also, since each item in the list has a reference to its predecessor and its successor, the items need not be stored consecutively in memory. The price we pay for these advantages is the overhead in creating each item in the list and in adding and deleting items from the list. Notice that each pair of adjacent items in a doubly linked list contains a circular reference!

In a large application, there may be many references to items in the list. It is the responsibility of each module of code to release its own references to these items. However, this does not destroy the list. A convenient way to do this is to create a *Manager* class. We then create a single object of this class, as shown in Figure 1.8, and allow it to reference items in the list. The *Terminate* event for the *Manager* object contains code to break the links in the list.

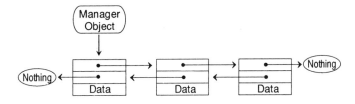

Figure 1.8

The key point is that we never allow any item in the list to reference the *Manager* object. Thus, the *Manager* object is never part of a circular reference involving items in the list. Hence, when all references to the *Manager* object are set to *Nothing,* the *Manager* object will be destroyed, bringing down with it the linked list, via the *Terminate* event.

Snippet 1.9 contains a portion of the code required to set up a doubly linked list.

Snippet 1.9 — A Doubly Linked List

The first class we need is *CItem*, whose objects are the items in the list. *CItem* has properties *NextItem*, *PrevItem* and *ItemData*. We code one method, named *InsertAfter*, to add an item to the list immediately following the item that called the method (*Me*).

```
' CItem Class
Public NextItem As CItem
Public PrevItem As CItem
Public ItemData As Integer

Public Function InsertAfter() As CItem

' Insert an item after the current item (Me)

Dim NewItem As New CItem

' If an item follows Me, then its PrevItem
' should now point to the new item
If Not (Me.NextItem Is Nothing) Then
    Set Me.NextItem.PrevItem = NewItem
End If

' NextItem of new item points to My NextItem
Set NewItem.NextItem = Me.NextItem

' PrevItem of new item points to Me
Set NewItem.PrevItem = Me

' My NextItem points to new item
Set Me.NextItem = NewItem
```

```
' Return the New Item so we can add the data
Set InsertAfter = NewItem

End Function

Private Sub Class_Terminate()
MsgBox "Destroying item. Data was: " & Me.ItemData
End Sub
```

The *CManager* class has three properties: *CurrentFirst* references the first item in the list; *CurrentItem* acts like a "read/write head" that moves along the list and is useful for searching the list, for instance; and *ListCt* keeps a count of the number of items in the list. The *AddItem* method adds a new item to the front of the list. This method is used to create the list initially. As mentioned before, the *Terminate* event contains code to break the circular links.

```
' CManager Class
Public CurrentFirst As CItem
Public CurrentItem As CItem
Public ListCt As Integer

Public Function AddItem() As CItem

' Add an item to the front of the list

Dim NewItem As New CItem
If Me.CurrentFirst Is Nothing Then
    ' If no CurrentFirst then list is empty
    Set Me.CurrentItem = NewItem
    Set Me.CurrentFirst = NewItem
Else
    ' List not empty
    ' Put new item at front of list
    Set Me.CurrentFirst.PrevItem = NewItem
    ' New item's next item is old CurrentFirst
    Set NewItem.NextItem = Me.CurrentFirst
    ' CurrentFirst is now new item
    Set Me.CurrentFirst = NewItem
End If

Me.ListCt = Me.ListCt + 1
```

```
' Return the new item so we can set its data field
Set AddItem = NewItem

End Function

Private Sub Class_Terminate()

' Remove all links (references) in the list
Dim ItemToFree As New CItem
Set Me.CurrentItem = Me.CurrentFirst

' Don't forget to remove this reference!
Set Me.CurrentFirst = Nothing

Do
    MsgBox " Unlinking item with data: " &
Me.CurrentItem.ItemData
    Set ItemToFree = Me.CurrentItem
    ' Prepare for next item
    Set Me.CurrentItem = Me.CurrentItem.NextItem
    ' Break item free
    Set ItemToFree.PrevItem = Nothing
    Set ItemToFree.NextItem = Nothing

Loop Until Me.CurrentItem Is Nothing

Set ItemToFree = Nothing

End Sub
```

Finally, we have the code for the *Form_Load* event in the main form. This code creates a small linked list with five items, containing the integer data 1, 2, 3, 5, 6. Then we demonstrate how to use the *Manager* class to insert an item in the list (with data value 4).

```
Private Sub Form_Load()

Dim i As Integer
Dim Manager As New CManager

' Create 5 item doubly linked list,
```

```
' with data 1-6, 4 missing for now
For i = 6 To 5 Step -1
    Manager.AddItem.ItemData = i
Next i
For i = 3 To 1 Step -1
    Manager.AddItem.ItemData = i
Next i

' Print list in debug window to verify
Debug.Print "Original list"
Set Manager.CurrentItem = Manager.CurrentFirst
For i = 1 To Manager.ListCt
    Debug.Print Manager.CurrentItem.ItemData
    Set Manager.CurrentItem =
Manager.CurrentItem.NextItem
Next i

Set Manager.CurrentItem = Manager.CurrentFirst

' Insert item with data 4 in list after the "3" item
For i = 1 To Manager.ListCt
    If Manager.CurrentItem.ItemData = "3" Then
        Manager.CurrentItem.InsertAfter.ItemData = "4"
        Manager.ListCt = Manager.ListCt + 1
        Exit For
    Else
        Set Manager.CurrentItem =
Manager.CurrentItem.NextItem
    End If
Next i

' Print list in debug window to verify
Debug.Print "New list"
Set Manager.CurrentItem = Manager.CurrentFirst
For i = 1 To Manager.ListCt
    Debug.Print Manager.CurrentItem.ItemData
    Set Manager.CurrentItem =
Manager.CurrentItem.NextItem
Next i

Stop    'Take a peek at the debug window

' Destroy the Manager and thereby break up the list
```

```
Set Manager = Nothing

End Sub
```

If you run this code, take a peek at the debug window when the *Stop* statement executes and you will see the data items before and after the insertion. Then let the program continue. You will see the following messages, indicating that each item in the list (starting from the front) has its links released and then, as soon as an item is no longer linked to other items in the list, that item is destroyed.

```
Unlinking item with data: 1
Unlinking item with data: 2
Destroying item. Data was: 1
Unlinking item with data: 3
Destroying item. Data was: 2
Unlinking item with data: 4
Destroying item. Data was: 3
Unlinking item with data: 5
Destroying item. Data was: 4
Unlinking item with data: 6
Destroying item. Data was: 5
Destroying item. Data was: 6
```

Form Modules

Form modules and class modules are closely related. The precise relationship between these two types of modules is not made clear in Visual Basic's documentation, and since the point is only an academic one, it is not terribly important. The main thing to keep in mind is that the two types of modules have important commonalities and important differences.

Perhaps the main similarity between the two is that a form module can contain properties and methods, just like a class module. Thus, we can define a class within a form module. The main difference is that a form module can have a visible interface, whereas a class module cannot.

Another difference between the two types of modules is that a form module has a *Name* property but it does not have an *Instancing* property nor a *Public* property, as does a class module. In other words, form modules cannot be made directly accessible to other applications, which makes sense because of the visual interface. (In a true multitasking environment, we generally don't want one program to cause another program to *display* information.)

Properties and Methods in a Form Module

As mentioned, the principal way in which a form module resembles a class module is that we can define properties and methods in a form module in exactly the same way as in a class module.

On the other hand, a new form module is more than a template for creating objects — it comes with an existing, built-in *Form* object. To see this, start a new project, which automatically creates a form module named *Form1*. Insert another form module, called *Form2,* and add to it a property and a method as follows:

```
'' (In Form2)
Public Form2Prop As String

Public Function Form2Fun() As Integer
Form2Fun = 5
End Function
```

Unlike a class module, and with no further ado, we can access the property and methods of *Form2*; to wit:

```
'' (In Form1_Load)
Form2.Form2Prop = "Donna"
MsgBox Form2.Form2Prop
MsgBox Form2.Form2Fun
```

It is possible to instance additional forms from an existing form module. For instance, the following creates a new instance of *Form2*, changes its caption and shows it:

```
Dim NewForm2 As Form2
Set NewForm2 = New Form2
NewForm2.Caption = "NewForm2"
NewForm2.Show
```

If you run the following code, you will see that *NewForm2*'s instance variable *Form2Prop* is empty (as it should be) and that *NewForm2*'s method *Form2Fun* returns 5, as expected, since the two instances share the same method code.

```
MsgBox NewForm2.Form2Prop
MsgBox NewForm2.Form2Fun
```

Collection Classes

Real-life applications may have hundreds, or even thousands, of objects alive at one time. To keep an object alive, that is, to keep Visual Basic from destroying it, the object's reference count must be at least one. This means hundreds or even thousands of references.

As we have seen, one way to keep a collection of objects alive is to use a linked list, where one object references another, which in turn references a third, and so on. However, this approach may not be convenient.

Fortunately, Visual Basic provides a special type of class, known as a *collection class*, specifically designed for storing objects. Since a reference is automatically kept to each object in the collection, we don't have to worry about keeping our own individual references.

The idea of a collection class is not special to Visual Basic. Most object-oriented programming languages implement some feature for maintaining groups of objects. In the general theory of object-oriented languages, the set of all instances of a given class in a running program is referred to as the *extent* (or *extension*) of the class. Some languages provide direct access to the extent of a class. However, Visual Basic does not.

Instead, Visual Basic provides collection classes which, in many cases, are more useful than extents. Collection classes provide not only a way to keep a collection of objects alive, but also a way to categorize objects, simply by placing them in different collections.

If you have been programming in Visual Basic, then you may have already used the built-in collections called *Forms* and *Controls*. The *Forms* collection holds the set of all *loaded* forms in a running project and the *Controls* collection for a given form holds the *loaded* controls on that form. If you are not familiar with these collections, you might want to try the following simple experiment.

Snippet 1.10

Create a new project and add an additional form, called *Form2*. In *Form1*, add a text box and a command button. In the *Form_Load* event of *Form1*, put the code

```
Private Form_Load()
Load Form2
MsgBox "Number of loaded forms: " & Forms.Count
MsgBox "Control count on Form1: " & _
   Form1.Controls.Count
End Sub
```

Run the project. You will get a message indicating that you have two loaded forms and then a message that *Form1* has two controls. You can also access each control using a loop, as follows:

```
' Declare a variable of type Control
Dim ctlVar as Control

For each ctlVar in Controls

   ' Set Top property to 0
   ctlVar.Top = 0

   ' Add text to text box
   If TypeOf ctlVar Is TextBox then
     ctlVar.Text = "Oh Boy"
   End If

Next ctlVar
```

This code will move all of the loaded controls on the current form to the top of the form's client area and put the text "Oh Boy" in the text box.

Collection objects can be created to hold objects of the more traditional data types; for instance, collections of integers or collections of strings. Also, unlike in some other object-oriented languages, in Visual Basic a single collection object can hold objects of different types, although this practice can easily lead to confusion. (Try it for yourself.)

As the Visual Basic documentation points out, some of the advantages of collections over arrays are

- A collection object may use less memory than an array.
- A collection object has more flexible indexing.
- A collection object provides easy methods for inserting and deleting items.
- A collection object automatically adjusts its size, eliminating the need to use a *ReDim* statement.

Constructing a Collection Class

Since a collection class is a just a special type of class, the first step in creating a collection class is to add a new class module to the project. Let us create a collection of students for our hypothetical teacher. Since this collection class will hold objects from the *CStudent* class, we will call it *CStudents*. It is customary, but by no means necessary, to name a collection with the plural of the name of the class whose objects will form the collection.

The distinction between a collection class and any other type of class may seem a bit confusing at first — but it is actually quite simple.

> A collection class is simply a class that has an object property of type *Collection*.

An object of type *Collection* is a special object that Visual Basic provides. It has a special property, called *Count*, to keep track of the number of objects in the collection, and special methods, such as *Add*, to add new objects to the collection.

Thus, it would be probably be less confusing to refer to a *collection class* as a *class with a collection object property*, but that is seldom done in practice. Nonetheless, it is the collection object property that "embodies" (and also manages) the collection.

Of course, there is more to the *proper* implementation of a collection class than just adding such a property, but let us begin with a simple, if not elegant, approach.

Snippet 1.11 — A Crude CStudent Collection Class

Start a new project and insert a class called *CStudent*. For illustration, we need only one property:

```
Public FullName As String
```

Insert a second class, which will be the collection class, and call it *CStudents*. This class contains only the object property of type *Collection*. Note the use of the *New* keyword in the declaration (below), to permit implicit creation of the *Collection* object *mCollection*. Note also that we are properly encapsulating the *Collection* property, exposing it through *Property Get* and *Property Set* methods. (More on this later.)

```
'' (In CStudents collection class)
Private mCollection As New Collection

Public Property Get Collection() As Collection
Set Collection = mCollection
End Property

Public Property Set Collection(pCollection As _
Collection)
Set mCollection = pCollection
End Property
```

You may also wish to note, in the code above, the use of the word *collection* in two different senses — as a property name and as a type identifier. This is referred to as *name overloading*. We will discuss this concept briefly later in the chapter.

That's it. We have created a collection class. To use the class, add the following code to the *Form_Load* event of the main form. This code adds two students to the *CStudents* collection and shows off the property (*Count*) and methods (*Add, Item*) of the *Collection* class. We will discuss these properties and methods in detail after the example.

```
Private Sub Form_Load()

' Define a new CStudents object
Dim objStudents As New CStudents

' Create a new student
Dim objStudent As CStudent
Set objStudent = New CStudent
objStudent.FullName = "Frederic Chopin"
```

```
' Add new student to the collection
objStudents.Collection.Add objStudent

' Another student
Set objStudent = New CStudent
objStudent.FullName = "Wolfgang Mozart"
objStudents.Collection.Add objStudent

' Show count
MsgBox objStudents.Collection.Count

' Show the first student's name
MsgBox objStudents.Collection.Item(1).FullName

' Iterate through collection
Dim objS As CStudent
For Each objS In objStudents.Collection
    MsgBox objS.FullName
Next objS

End Sub
```

Running this code will produce several message boxes. First we see the size of the collection, which is 2. Then we see the name of the first student in the collection. Then we see the names of each student in the collection. We have included the last group of messages simply to illustrate the use of the *For Each* *<object>* syntax, which is specially designed to trace through a collection (or an array).

The Properties and Methods of a Collection Object

Before turning this example into a proper implementation of a collection class, we need to discuss the properties and methods of a *Collection* object (that is, an object of type *Collection*). Note that these properties and methods are *built-in*. That is, Visual Basic provides them for us as soon as we define an object of type *Collection*. However, they contain no validation code, so we must take on that duty ourselves, as we will see in a moment.

The *Collection* class has a single built-in (read-only) property called *Count* that returns the number of objects in the class. The built-in methods of the *Collection* class are *Add*, *Remove* and *Item*.

The *Add* method allows us to add new objects to the collection and has the syntax

```
CollectionObject.Add Item, Key, Before, After
```

where *item* is a variable that refers to the object to be added to the collection, and the optional *key* is a unique string expression that can be used to identify the object. Without the key, an object could be accessed only by its position in the collection (first, second, third,. . .). The optional *before* and *after* parameters are used for positioning the item in the collection.

The *Item* method has the syntax

```
CollectionObject.Item vKey
```

This method returns the object indicated by *vKey*. The parameter has type *Variant* because Visual Basic lets us to ask for an item either by its string ID (the *key* value from the *Add* method) or by its ordinal position (an integer) in the collection. (Note that the first item in a *user-defined* collection has index 1, but the first item in the built-in *Forms* and *Controls* collections has index 0.)

What's Wrong with Our First Attempt

Now let us discuss what is wrong with the previous implementation of a collection class. The problem is a bit subtle. Namely, Visual Basic has thoughtfully provided us with built-in methods, such as the *Add* method, but of course, it could not provide us with validation code, since Visual Basic does not know how we intend to use the method!

Now, even though we have carefully adhered to good encapsulation rules by declaring the *Collection* property as *private*

```
'' (In CStudents collection class)
Private mCollection As New Collection
```

and exposing it through *Property Get* and *Property Set* methods, there is an "encapsulation leak." To wit, we cannot add validation code to the *Add* method, since it is built into Visual Basic.

Put more crudely, even though we can add validation code to the *Property Get* and *Property Set* methods of the *Collection* property, once a programmer has his or her hands on this property, we can't control how he or she uses the *Add* method (nor the other methods).

To illustrate the problem, try the following experiment, which adds an object to the *CStudents* collection that is not of type *CStudent*!

Snippet 1.12 — A Ringer in the Collection Class

Insert an additional class module into the project and call it *CFake*. Add the property declaration

```
Public FakeName As String
```

Change the *Form_Load* event to add an object of type *CFake* to the collection, as follows:

```
Private Sub Form_Load()

' Define a new CStudents object
Dim objStudents As New CStudents
Dim i As Integer

' Create a new student
Dim objStudent As CStudent
Set objStudent = New CStudent
objStudent.FullName = "Frederic Chopin"

' Add new Student to the collection
objStudents.Collection.Add objStudent

' Another student
Set objStudent = New CStudent
objStudent.FullName = "Wolfgang Mozart"
objStudents.Collection.Add objStudent

' Add fake
Dim objFake As New CFake
objFake.FakeName = "fake name"
objStudents.Collection.Add objFake
```

```
' Show count
MsgBox objStudents.Collection.Count

' Use For loop and TypeOf to display names
For i = 1 To objStudents.Collection.Count
  If TypeOf objStudents.Collection.Item(i) Is _
    CStudent Then
    MsgBox objStudents.Collection.Item(i).FullName
  ElseIf TypeOf objStudents.Collection.Item(i) Is _
    CFake Then
    MsgBox objStudents.Collection.Item(i).FakeName
  End If
Next i

End Sub
```

Running the previous code displays a count of 3 and the names of each of the three objects in the collection, including the object of type *CFake*. Note that we have used a *For* loop along with the *TypeOf* keyword in order to list the names of the objects, since they are referred to by different identifiers (*FullName* and *FakeName*).

The Solution to the Problem — Wrapper Methods

The solution to the problem described above is both simple and elegant. In particular, it is clear from what we have seen that we cannot allow general access to the *Collection* property; that is, we must not expose the *Collection* property — even through *Property Let* and *Property Get* methods. This is where implicit object creation comes to our rescue, for we can use it to ask a *CStudents* collection object to create its own *private Collection* property.

Let us go through the individual pieces of code needed to properly implement the collection class. Then we will collect all of the code together in one place for easy reading.

We begin by declaring the *Collection* property as *Private*, and preparing for implicit creation with the *New* keyword.

```
'' (In CStudents collection class)
Private mStudents As New Collection
```

Note that we have also changed the variable name to reflect the context and prefixed an "m" for member variable.

Next, we expose the *built-in* properties and methods of the *Collection* class by creating our own methods that first validate and then call the built-in methods! Our methods are referred to as *wrapper methods*, because they *wrap* the built-in methods with a layer of additional code.

To expose the *Count* property, we just use an ordinary *Property Get* method:

```
Public Property Get Count() As Long
Count = mStudents.Count
End Property
```

The wrapper for the *Item* method needs no validation, since we are just retrieving the object:

```
Public Function Item(vKey As Variant) As CStudent
Set Item = mStudents.Item(vKey)
End Function
```

Exposing the Add Method

Wrapping Visual Basic's *Add* method is a bit more involved. Since adding an object to a collection is done using the key value, a decision first has to be made about what to use for that value, which must be unique to each object in the collection. If there is a unique property or combination of properties, this can serve as a key.

Just to illustrate, imagine a class *CCircle*, whose objects are circles. Each circle has two properties: *center* and *radius*. Together, these properties uniquely identify the circle, and so we could use a combination of them as the key value, as in

```
colCircles.Add objCircle, objCircle.Center & _
objCircle.Radius
```

In our example, the *StudentID* property could serve as a key value. When no obvious key presents itself, the strategy is to make up a key. For purposes of illustration, let us ignore the obvious key in this case and describe the procedure for creating an artificial key.

Code for the artificial key needs to be added to the *CStudent* class (not to the *CStudents* collection class), as shown below. Note the implementation of the ID property as a *write-once* property. This is done by declaring a *static* variable to keep track of whether the ID property has already been set. This works *precisely* because all instances of a class share the same method code. This practice is not, strictly speaking, necessary — but it is elegant. (Incidentally, don't use mID for the ID member variable name, because the Visual Basic editor will change all references to the MID$ function/statement to mID$!)

Snippet 1.13 — The CStudent Class Again

```
' Add to the CStudent Class

Private m_ID As String

Public Property Let ID(pID As String)
' A write-once property
Static bAlreadySet As Boolean
If Not bAlreadySet Then
    m_ID = pID
    bAlreadySet = True
End If
End Property

Public Property Get ID() As String
ID = m_ID
End Property
```

With the necessary code in place in the *CStudent* class module, we must include some additional code for the ID property in the *CStudents* collection class. This amounts to nothing more than a *private* function that gets the "next" available ID string, and so we can use it in the *Add* method. The simplest procedure is to use an integer variable, increment it by one each time the function is called and then convert it to a string.

```
Private Function NextID() As String

' Get the next available ID string
```

```
Static iNextAvail As Integer

iNextAvail = iNextAvail + 1
NextID = "ID" & Format$(iNextAvail, "00000")

End Function
```

Now we are ready for the wrapper for the *Add* method. As is customary, we also use the name *Add* for the wrapper method. In particular, our *Add* method creates the new *CStudent* object, sets its properties using the parameters of the method and then adds it to the collection, using Visual Basic's built-in *Add* method. As is also customary, our function is designed to return the object added, which allows for easy access to the new object, in case additional properties need to be set (or for other reasons).

```
Public Function Add(FullName As String, StudentID _
As String, Optional Before As Variant, Optional _
After As Variant) As CStudent

' Implicitly define a new CStudent object
Dim lStudent As New CStudent

With lStudent

   ' Set properties
   .FullName = FullName
   .StudentID = StudentID
   .ID = NextID

   ' Add to collection
   mStudents.Add lStudent, lStudent.ID, Before,_
   After

End With

' Return the object added
Set Add = lStudent

End Function
```

There are a few other things to note about the code for the *Add* wrapper method. First, we have used the *With* <object> ..*End With* construct, which makes it convenient to set several properties for a single object. Also, we deliberately used unadulterated names for the parameters of the *Add* function, since this function supports *named arguments*. Thus, we can call the *Add* method using a syntax such as

```
colStudents.Add StudentID:="12345", FullName:= _
  "F. Chopin"
```

without having to worry about the order of the parameters (and, hopefully, without having to refer back to the function declaration to recall the parameter names).

Let us collect the entire *CStudents* collection class code in one place, for easier perusal. We have also exposed the *Remove* method and included an additional method to clear the contents of the entire collection.

Snippet 1.14 — The CStudents Collection Class

```
'  The CStudents collection class

' Declare a variable of type collection
Private mStudents as New Collection

' Expose Count property
Public Property Get Count() As Long
Count = mStudents.Count
End Property

' Wrapper for Item method
Public Function Item(vKey As Variant) As CStudent
Set Item = mStudents.Item(vKey)
End Function

' Private function to get next ID
Private Function NextID() As String
' Get the next available ID string
Static iNextAvail As Integer
iNextAvail = iNextAvail + 1
NextID = "ID" & Format$(iNextAvail, "00000")
End Function
```

```vb
' Wrapper for Add method
Public Function Add(FullName As String, StudentID As
String) As CStudent

' Define a new CStudent object
Dim lStudent As New CStudent

With lStudent

    ' Set properties
    .FullName = FullName
    .StudentID = StudentID
    .ID = NextID

    ' Add to collection
    mStudents.Add lStudent, lStudent.ID

End With

' Return the object added
Set Add = lStudent

End Function

Public Sub Remove(vID As Variant)
'Remove a new member from collection
' vID can be the string ID or the position
' of the item in the class
mStudents.Remove vID
End Sub

Public Sub Clear()
' Clear the entire class
Set mStudents = Nothing
End Sub
```

To use the *CStudents* collection class, we first create a collection object of type *CStudents* (say in the *Form_Load* event):

```vb
'' (In Form_Load event)
Dim colStudents as CStudents
```

```
Set colStudents = New CStudents
```

Adding to the *colStudents* collection is quite easy. Let us give two new students, named Wolfgang and Frederic, the *StudentID*'s 111-111-11 and 222-222-22, respectively. (Don't confuse these IDs with the IDs for the collection key, which are assigned by the *NextID* function in the *Add* method).

```
colStudents.Add FullName:="Wolfgang Mozart", _
StudentID:="111-111-11"

colStudents.Add FullName:="Frederic Chopin", _
StudentID:="222-222-22"
```

Note that the first line of the code above causes the first use of the instance variable *mStudents*, in the *CStudents* collection class, resulting in the implicit creation of our collection object.

Next, we display the collection's *Count* property (which is 2). The *Item* method can be used in either of two ways — either it takes an integer variable denoting the position of the object in the collection, or it takes a string variable denoting the key value of the object, as shown below

```
MsgBox colStudents.Count
MsgBox colStudents.Item(1).FullName
MsgBox colStudents.Item("ID00002").FullName
```

Note that Visual Basic will adjust the ordinal position of objects within the collection as new objects are inserted or deleted. Thus, some care must be taken when relying on these positions. (Perhaps it is better *not* to rely on this index to find a *specific* item.)

The following code inserts a new student "between" Wolfgang and Frederic:

```
colStudents.Add FullName:="Bill Schumann", _
StudentID:="333-333-33", After:="ID00001"
```

Now we can take a look at the entire list, in order:

```
For i = 1 To colStudents.Count
  MsgBox colStudents.Item(i).FullName & "-" & _
    colStudents.Item(i).ID
Next I
```

Finally, if you want to list the items in the *CStudent* collection in a list box, for instance, you could create a *ListBox* control on the main form and then add the following method to the *CStudents* collection. Note the use of the *For Each* syntax.

```
Public Sub ListStudents()

Form1.List1.Clear

' Declare a new student to use in the For Each loop
Dim lStudent As New CStudent

For Each lStudent In mStudents
    Form1.List1.AddItem lStudent.FullName & "-" & _
    lStudent.StudentID
Next lStudent

' Be neat
Set lStudent = Nothing

End Sub
```

Then, in the *Form_Load* event, we make a call to this method (and show the form):

```
colStudents.ListStudents
Me.Show
```

Note that, as soon as the *Form_Load* method terminates, the collection object variable *colStudents* will go out of scope and so the collection object will be destroyed. Thus, it is probably not a good idea to put the above code in the *Form_Load* event. We have done so only as an expediency, to simplify the examples. We may even want to declare the *colStudents* variable as *Public* (in a standard module) to keep it alive during the entire life of the application.

A Note About the For Each Syntax

The *For Each* syntax is very compelling, but there seems to be a bit of confusion about when it can (and cannot) be used. At first, it might seem as though we could put code such as the following in, say, the *Form_Load* event:

```
Dim colStudents as CStudents
Dim lStudent As New CStudent
For Each lStudent In colStudents
    Form1.List1.AddItem lStudent.FullName & "-" & _
    lStudent.StudentID
Next lStudent
```

The Visual Basic Help documentation states that, in the syntax

```
For Each <Element> In <Group>
```

the term *Group* is the "Name of an object collection . . .". This terminology is
a bit confusing and might seem to suggest that, since *colStudents* is a variable
that refers to an object collection (i.e., collection of objects), the preceding
code should work. However, it just generates the error message "*Object
doesn't support this property or method.*"

The fact is that Visual Basic requires *Group* to be a variable of type
Collection, as in

```
Private mStudents as New Collection
```

and not of type *CStudents* (which is a collection class), as in

```
Dim colStudents as CStudents
```

In other words, *Group* must be the name of a *Collection* object, *not* the name
of an object collection!

As a consequence, the *For Each* syntax is most useful when it appears
within the collection class itself, where a *private* variable of type *Collection* is
declared, in keeping with the principles of encapsulation.

Polymorphism and Overloading

We want to conclude this chapter by discussing a few object-oriented concepts
that are, strictly speaking, of a more academic interest than a practical interest
to Visual Basic programmers. These are *polymorphism* and *inheritance*. Our
discussion will be brief, but you may feel free to skip this discussion without
compromising your understanding of later material.

If you have looked into object-oriented programming before, you may have seen the terms *polymorphism* and *overloading*. While the terms have similar meanings, the two concepts are not the same. Before proceeding, we should point out that there is not complete agreement among computer scientists on how these terms should be defined. However, since we don't actually need to *use* these concepts, our goal here is just to convey the general idea.

Overloading

The concept of overloading is pretty straightforward. An identifier (symbol or name) is said to be *overloaded* if it takes on more than one meaning. For instance, the plus sign + refers to addition of integers, addition of singles, addition of doubles and concatenation of strings. Thus, the symbol + is *overloaded*. It's a good thing, too, for otherwise we would need separate symbols for adding integers, singles and doubles. (We do have a different symbol for concatenation of strings — the ampersand.)

You may also hear it (incorrectly) said that the *operator* + is overloaded, but it is really the symbol (or the name *addition*) that has many meanings. There is one operation for each such meaning.

Function names can also be overloaded. For instance, the absolute value function name *Abs* can take an integer parameter, or a single parameter, or a double parameter. Because the name *Abs* represents several *different* functions, it is overloaded.

Overloading is very common and not at all unique to object-oriented programming.

Polymorphism

In a general sense, the term *polymorphism* means *having or passing through many different forms*. In the world of computer languages, it has several meanings, and computer scientists do not seem to be in total agreement on a proper definition of the term.

In any case, there are various forms of polymorphism. Some computer scientists say that overloading is a form of polymorphism, and some say it is not.

A variable is *polymorphic* if it can hold more than one type of data at different times. Nothing could describe better a variable of type *Variant* in Visual Basic. To see this, try the following simple experiment. In a new project, enter and run the code

```
Dim vtest As Variant
vtest = 3
MsgBox TypeName(vtest)
vtest = 3.3
MsgBox TypeName(vtest)
vtest = "test"
MsgBox TypeName(vtest)
```

You will get three message boxes, containing the messages "integer," "double" and "string." Thus, the variant *vTest* can take many forms.

Another example of a polymorphic variable in Visual Basic is the generic *Object* variable. We will have much to say about this variable in the chapter on OLE automation, but for now, consider the following legal code:

```
Dim obj As Object
Set obj = New Class1
obj.Prop1 = 4
MsgBox obj.Prop1

Set obj = New Class2
obj.Prop2 = 5
MsgBox obj.Prop2
```

In this case, the project has two classes — *Class1* and *Class2* — each with its own integer property. By declaring a variable to be of type *Object*, that variable can hold objects of both classes at different times. Hence, it is polymorphic.

A function is *polymorphic* if it can take different parameter types at different times. As an example, consider the function *Second*, defined by

```
Function Second(x as Integer, y as Integer) _
   As Integer
Second = y
End Function
```

This function is *not* polymorphic, since it can take only integer parameters. But we can make it into a polymorphic function as follows:

```
Function Second(x as Variant, y as Variant) _
   As Variant
Second = y
End Function
```

Now the function *Second* can take integer parameters, single parameters, string parameters and so on. It is therefore polymorphic.

Note the difference between an overloaded function name and a polymorphic function. In the former case, a single function *name* represents several *different* functions (that is, different code), whereas in the latter case, a *single* function (the same code) can take several different parameters.

Inheritance

The concept of *inheritance* is one of the most important in the theory of object-oriented programming. We can illustrate the issue quite simply with an example. Consider a class *CStudent*, which has three properties (*Exam1*, *Exam2* and *Exam3*) and one method (*Average*).

Suppose we wish also to include a class called *CGiftedStudent* in our application. This class should have the same properties and methods as the class *CStudent*, as well as some additional properties, such as *StudentIQ*, and some additional methods, such as *AdvancedPlacementAverage*.

Now, to construct the new class in Visual Basic, we need to insert a new class module and implement *all* of the properties and methods for *CGiftedStudent*. This means adding duplicates of the properties and method of the class *CStudent*. However, in C++, for instance, we could write

```
class CGiftedStudent : CStudent
```

which has the effect that every object of class *CGiftedStudent* automatically *inherits* the properties and methods of class *CStudent*. It would then be necessary only to define the *new* properties and methods in the *CGiftedStudent* class module.

In this case, we say that *CGiftedStudent inherits from CStudent*. The class *CGiftedStudent* is referred to as the *derived class*, and *CStudent* is the *base class*. Also, we say that *CGiftedStudent* is a *subclass* of *CStudent* and that *CStudent* is a *superclass* of *CGiftedStudent*.

The concept of inheritance can get quite involved. For instance, it may be useful for a subclass to inherit only some of the properties and methods of the base class, or to be able to *redefine*, or *override*, some of these properties and methods. In some languages, a class can inherit from more than one superclass. This is referred to as *multiple inheritance*. Also, inheritance can be at odds with encapsulation. If an object of the subclass has direct access to its instance variables in the superclass, we have a violation of encapsulation.

On the other hand, inheritance has a great many virtues, including such obvious things as code reusability, since the code for the method written in the superclass need not be rewritten in the subclass.

Note also that inheritance leads to polymorphism. For instance, the *Average* method now applies not just to parameters of type *CStudent*, but also to parameters of type *CGiftedStudent*. This can cause complications.

While Visual Basic does not currently support inheritance, it is true that some of the features of inheritance can be duplicated without explicit use of the technique. For instance, we could add a Boolean property to the *CStudent* class called *IsGifted*, to indicate which students are gifted. We could then implement the *AdvancedPlacementAverage* method with some code to prevent it from returning a value when *IsGifted* is false. This approach may work for small applications but may not be a workable option for applications with large numbers of classes and methods.

Chapter 2
Handling Object Errors

Let us now turn to the subject of error handling. This important subject can seem quite complicated and confusing at times (an *imbroglio*, if you will), and so our goal is to attempt to put some order in this apparent confusion. Once the options have been clearly defined, you may find that error handling is not as unpleasant as many programmers seem to feel.

Incidentally, the subject of error handling is certainly not unique to object-oriented programming, but Visual Basic is kind enough to give the subject an object-oriented flavor by providing us with a built-in object called the *error object*. This is my excuse to include a chapter on error handling in a book that is devoted to object-oriented programming. However, in order to present a coherent picture of error-handling techniques, we will start at the beginning.

Error Detection and Error Handling

The place to begin is by clarifying some terminology. Let us agree to say that *handling* an error means executing some form of response to a *detected* error.

There are three levels at which errors can be handled. The weakest form of error handling is to present the user with an error message, however informative, and then terminate the application. This is generally what happens with *unanticipated* run-time errors, such as dividing by 0. Some programmers might not want to think of this as error handling at all, but it is certainly better than just terminating the application with no message. In particular, the message may help the programmer determine the source of the error.

At the other extreme, some errors can be handled by fixing the error in code without bothering the user at all. For instance, if a program requires a string of uppercase letters from a user, the problem of entering lowercase letters can be handled as follows:

```
Response = InputBox("Enter an uppercase string.")
Response = UCase$(Response)
```

However, most error handling involves both informing the user of the error and asking whether he or she wants to correct the error or cancel the operation that caused the error. Indeed, few errors are amenable to handling with no user intervention. The user usually needs to do something, such as change the input, put a floppy disk in the drive, swap floppy disks and so on. If an error results, for instance, from the user's inputting a negative number instead of a positive one, then it would be foolhardy for the programmer to assume that the user intended to input the absolute value of the number! The only proper response is to inform the user of the problem and ask for fresh input.

Of course, before an error can be handled, it must be *detected*. Certainly, many errors, such as dividing by 0, force their attention upon us. But others, such as the error of entering lowercase letters instead of uppercase letters, require that we deliberately check for them, or else we may suffer the consequences sometime down the road.

One reason to make a clear distinction between *error detection* and *error handling* (as we will do) is that these processes can take place at different times and in different locations within the code of an application.

Let us agree to refer to the procedure (or module) in which an error occurs as the *offending* procedure (or module).

Types of Errors

There are two types of errors that can occur in a *running* program. (We will not discuss *compile-time* errors.) A *run-time error* occurs when Visual Basic attempts to perform an operation that is impossible to perform, such as opening a file that does not exist, or dividing by 0. Visual Basic automatically takes care of error detection for run-time errors, because it has no other choice. On the other hand, *proper* error handling of run-time errors is up to the programmer, for otherwise Visual Basic will handle the error, by presenting an error message and terminating the application, which is not a good solution to the problem.

A *logical error* is often defined as the production of an *unexpected* result. It might be better to define it as the production of an unexpected and *incorrect* result (although even this is still somewhat ambiguous). For instance, consider a function that returns a student's grade for a course. If the student has been doing very well in the course, we might expect that the student will get an "A." A grade of "B" might be unexpected, but it not necessarily an error. On the other hand, if the function returns a grade of "Z," *that* is a logical error.

Visual Basic does not provide error detection for logical errors, because to Visual Basic, no error has occurred (yet). However, a logical error may subsequently result in a run-time error, which Visual Basic will certainly recognize. For instance, code that is intended to retrieve a positive integer into an integer variable for later use may instead retrieve 0. This is a logical error. But if that integer is used later *as a denominator* in some other part of the application, we can surely expect a run-time error!

Thus, it is up to the programmer to anticipate logical errors and provide both error detection and error handling. From this perspective, logical errors are more serious, and more difficult to deal with, than run-time errors. After all, a run-time error is not going to be *completely* overlooked — at least Visual Basic will do something about it, even if that consists only of presenting an error message to the user and terminating the application.

The problem with an overlooked logical error is that it may give the user *specious* information (that is, *invalid* information that *looks valid*). This is no doubt the most insidious behavior a program can produce. If we are lucky, a logical error will generate a run-time error at some later date, but we may still have great difficulty determining the location of the logical error from the run-time error message.

The Error Object

Visual Basic's built-in *error object*, called *Err*, is one of the main tools for error handling. This object has several properties, but we will be concerned only with the properties *Number*, *Description* and *Source*. The *Number* property is the number of the error and, for compatibility reasons, is the default property of the *Err* object. Thus, the code

```
If Err = 12 then ...
```

from an earlier version of Visual Basic is equivalent to

```
If Err.Number = 12 then ...
```

The *Description* property is a string property that describes the error. The *Source* property is a string property that describes the object that originally generated the error. This is usually the object's class name. (For an OLE automation error, it is the *programmatic ID*, which has the form *application.objectname*.)

The *Err* object has two methods. The *Clear* method clears the values of all properties of the *Err* object. The *Raise* method has the syntax

```
Err.Raise(Number, Source, Description, HelpFile,_
   HelpContext)
```

where all but the first named argument is optional. This method causes Visual Basic to generate a run-time error and sets the properties of the *Err* object to the values given by the parameters of the *Raise* method.

Dealing with Run-Time Errors

Visual Basic treats the programmer very courteously when it comes to run-time errors: It detects the error as soon as it happens; it saves information about the error by setting the properties of the *Err* object; and it directs the flow of execution to the location that the programmer specifies in the most recent *On Error* statement. This is outlined in the following code:

```
Function Example() as Variant

On Error Goto ErrHandler

'' If run-time error occurs here
'' Visual Basic directs execution to ErrHandler

Exit Function

ErrHandler:

'' Code can be placed here to handle errors
'' or pass them up the calls list.
'' We have knowledge of Err.Number, Err.Description,
'' and Err.Source.

Exit Function
```

`End Function`

Figure 2.1 shows models of the error-detecting/handling process for run-time errors. In both cases, code in the *CStudent* class calls a method in the *CReportCard* class. At some point, a run-time error occurs in that method.

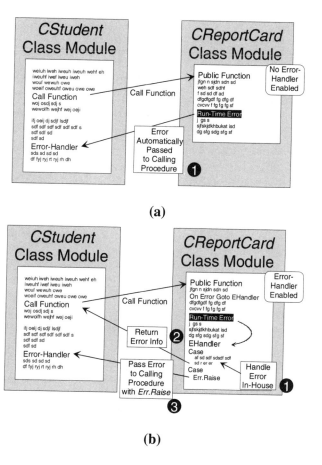

(a)

(b)

Figure 2.1

If, as shown in Figure 2.1a, there is no enabled error-handler in the offending procedure (that is, no *On Error* statement), then Visual Basic will automatically send the error to the calling procedure's error-handler. If the calling procedure has no error-handler, the error will continue up the calls list until it reaches an enabled error-handler. If none is found, then Visual Basic will handle the error by displaying an error message and terminating the application.

On the other hand, if, as in Figure 2.1b, the offending procedure has an enabled error-handler, then Visual Basic directs program execution to that handler, where there are several possibilities for dealing with the error, as shown by numbered circles in the figure. The error can be either handled in the error-handler or passed to the calling procedure.

One way to pass the error is to make the call

```
Err.Raise Err.Number
```

This will trigger the calling procedure's error-handler (or rather, the next enabled error-handler in the calls list). It will also pass the description of the error in *Err.Description* and the source of the error in *Err.Source* (provided the latter is an object). Hence, the calling procedure has all the information it needs to handle the error. This process is called *regenerating* or *reraising* the error.

Another approach is to pass information about an error to the calling procedure without invoking its error-handler. This can be done using parameters or in the return value of the function.

Let us consider these matters in more detail, with examples.

Where to Handle a Run-Time Error

Once execution reaches the error-handler, we need to decide whether to handle the error in the current procedure or pass information about the error to the calling procedure and let it decide what to do. The latter is often referred to as *passing* the error.

It is important to keep in mind that the calling program may pass the error further up the calls list and, indeed, will definitely do so if it is not *expecting* any errors and has therefore not enabled error detection with its own *On Error* statement. This may result in the error reaching an unexpected error-handler, or even in Visual Basic having to handle the error itself.

Passing the Error to the Calling Procedure

A run-time error can be passed to the calling program in a variety of ways:

- Pass the error in a public variable.
- Pass the error as a *ByRef* parameter of the offending function.

- Pass the error as the value of the offending function.
- Reraise the error in the active error-handler, using the *Err.Raise* method.

Note that another alternative is to prevent the error from going to the error-handler in the offending procedure by temporarily disabling error handling with the statement *On Error Goto 0*. If an error occurs, Visual Basic will automatically send it up the calls list. This approach is a bit dangerous, however, since we may forget to reenable error handling.

Defining a public variable to hold error information is not very object-oriented, since it flies in the face of encapsulation. So no more of it.

Passing the error as the value of a parameter is accomplished by adding an additional formal parameter to the procedure definition and setting that parameter to a value that indicates the nature of the error. Note that we must pass the parameter *by reference* (which is the default method) so that the procedure can change its value, thus giving the calling procedure access to the information. Let us illustrate this with a simple example that retrieves a number from the user and divides it into 100.

```
Public Sub DoDivide(pReturnMsg as string)

On Error Goto ErrDoDivide

pReturnMsg = "No error"
Denom = Val(InputBox("Enter denominator."))

NewVal = 100/Denom

Exit Sub

ErrDoDivide:
Select Case Err.Number
  Case 11  'Divide by 0
    pReturnMsg = "Divide by 0"
  Case Else
    pReturnMsg = "Unknown error"
End Select
Exit Sub

End Sub
```

This procedure could then be called with code such as

```
Dim ReturnMsg As String
DoDivide ReturnMsg
If ReturnMsg = "Divide by 0" then ...
```

The next possibility is to pass the error as the value of the function in which it occurred. This is easily done by setting the return type of the function to *Variant* so we can return a normal value when there is no error or a special value when there is an error. One difficulty is that these two values may have the same type, which could cause confusion on the calling end. Is a string returned by the function a value of the function or an error message?

To deal with this problem, we can take advantage of Visual Basic's *IsError* function to check for an error code. This involves a three-step process — first we convert the value of *Err.Number* to an error code using the *CVErr* type conversion function, then we return this error code to the calling procedure and finally, we test the value at the other end. Here is an example. Note that we have converted our subroutine to a function that returns a *Variant*.

```
Public Function DoDivide() As Variant

On Error Goto ErrDoDivide

Denom = Val(InputBox("Enter denominator."))

DoDivide =   100/Denom

Exit Function

ErrDoDivide:
' Convert error number to error code
' and return it as value of function
DoDivide = CVErr(Err.Number)
Exit Function

End Function
```

In the calling routine, we have

```
' Call function
Dim ReturnValue as Variant
ReturnValue = DoDivide
```

```
' Check return value type
If IsError(ReturnValue) then
   '' Deal with the error -
   '' We have the error number in ReturnValue
   '' and can get the description via
   '' Error$(CInt(ReturnValue))
End If
```

In using this technique, it is important to note that the only record of the error that reaches the calling routine is the value of the function (in this case *ReturnValue*). This is because the *Err* object is cleared when the function *DoDivide* is terminated. To retrieve a description of the error, we use the code

```
Error$(CInt(ReturnValue))
```

The final approach to passing an error to the calling routine is the simplest, and most elegant, of all. Just reraise the error in the active error-handler. Since an error-handler is disabled when it is active (executing), an error that occurs in an active error-handler (whether accidental or deliberate) will be passed up the calls list. *Voilà*.

```
Public Function DoDivide() As Variant

On Error Goto ErrDoDivide

Denom = Val(InputBox("Enter denominator."))

DoDivide =  100/Denom

Exit Function

ErrDoDivide:
Err.Raise Number:= Err.Number
Exit Function

End Function
```

Note that the calling routine will receive this error, along with the correct values of *Err.Description* and *Err.Source*.

Dealing with Logical Errors

Since Visual Basic makes the handling of run-time errors a relatively straightforward process, it seems reasonable to try to mimic this process for logical errors. Figure 2.2 show various possibilities for logical error handling.

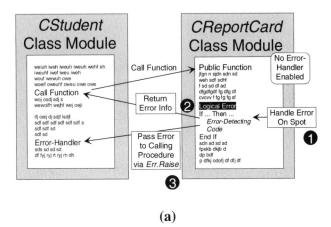

(a)

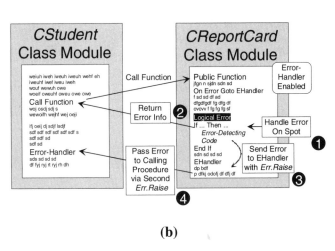

(b)

Figure 2.2

Detecting Logical Errors

To detect logical errors as soon as they occur, we place error-detection code immediately following the potential offender. For instance, consider the following procedure shell for getting a sequence of positive integers from the user, starting with the number of integers:

```
Public Sub GetSomeData()

DataCt = CInt(InputBox("Enter number of items."))

'' Code here to get the individual data values ...

End Sub
```

The proper place for error-detecting code is immediately following the *InputBox* statement, where we can check for a nonpositive integer.

```
Public Sub GetSomeData()

DataCt = CInt(InputBox("Enter number of items."))

' Check for error
If DataCt < = 0 then
    '' something here
End If

'' Code here to get the individual data values ...

End Sub
```

The alternative is to place error-detecting code just prior to *using* the value of *DataCt*, but this is dangerous and inefficient. It is dangerous since we might forget to place the code, and it is inefficient since we may use *DataCt* in a variety of locations in the program, each of which would require error-detecting code.

Where to Handle a Logical Error

Once a logical error is detected, we have three choices as to where to handle that error.

Handling the Error on the Spot

A logical error can be handled at the location where it was detected. Here is an example:

```
Public Sub GetSomeData()

TryAgain:

DataCt = CInt(InputBox("Enter number of items."))

' Check for error
If DataCt < = 0 then

   If MsgBox("Number must be a positive integer." & _
   " Try again or cancel.", vbQuestion+vbOKCancel) _
   = vbOK then

     Goto TryAgain

   Else
     Exit Sub
   End If

End If

'' Code here to get the individual data values ...

End Sub
```

Handling a logical error on the spot may be appropriate when the code required is short. It is also appropriate in *Property Let* and *Property Set* procedures, which often amount to little more than a single line that sets a private instance variable, preceded by data validation, which is essentially logical error detection.

Handling the Error in the Offending Procedure's Error-Handler

There is much to be said for centralizing error-handling code, especially when there is a lot of it. We can duplicate the procedure that Visual Basic uses for run-time errors simply by raising our own run-time error with the *Err.Raise* method. In effect, we *trade in* a logical error for a run-time error.

```
Public Sub GetSomeData()

On Error Goto ErrGetSomeData

DataCt = CInt(InputBox("Enter number of items."))

' Check for error
If DataCt < = 0 then

   ' Raise an error
   Err.Raise Number:= ErrBadDataCt

End If

'' Code here to get the individual data values ...

Exit Sub

' Error-handler
ErrGetSomeData:
Select Case Err.Number
  Case ErrBadDataCt
     '' Deal with this error by displaying
     '' message and getting help from user
  Case Else
     '' Deal with other errors
End Select
Exit Sub

End Sub
```

Passing the Error to the Calling Procedure

As with run-time errors, passing the error to the calling procedure can be done in several ways:

- Pass the error in a public variable.
- Pass the error as a *ByRef* parameter of the offending function.
- Pass the error as the value of the offending function.
- Raise the error (perhaps twice) using the *Err.Raise* method.

The last method acquires a new wrinkle with logical errors. Since Visual Basic does not raise an error in response to a logical error, the first time we call *Err.Raise*, execution will be directed to the most recently enabled error-handler. Thus, if the offending procedure has an enabled error-handler, we must either temporarily disable it with an *On Error Goto 0* statement, so the error will be sent up the calls list, or else *reraise* the same error in the error-handling routine, with a second call to *Err.Raise*. The latter is safer because we do not risk forgetting to reenable error handling in the offending procedure.

Here is the necessary code to temporarily turn off error handling and raise the error:

```
Public Sub GetSomeData()

On Error Goto ErrGetSomeData

DataCt = CInt(InputBox("Enter number of items."))

' Check for error
If DataCt < = 0 then

    ' Turn error handling off and raise error
    On Error Goto 0
    Err.Raise Number:= ErrBadDataCt
    ' Turn error handling on
    On Error Goto ErrGetSomeData

End If

'' Code here to get the individual data values ...

Exit Sub

' Error-handler
ErrGetSomeData:
'' Code here to handle other errors
Exit Sub

End Sub
```

Here is the code to raise the error twice:

```
Public Sub GetSomeData()
```

```
On Error Goto ErrGetSomeData

DataCt = CInt(InputBox("Enter number of items."))

' Check for error
If DataCt < = 0 then
  ' Raise an error
  Err.Raise Number:= ErrBadDataCt
End If

'' Code here to get the individual data values ...

Exit Sub

' Error-handler
ErrGetSomeData:
Select Case Err.Number
  Case ErrBadDataCt
    ' Raise this error again
    Err.Raise Number:= ErrBadDataCt
  Case Else
    '' Deal with other errors
End Select
Exit Sub

End Sub
```

Error Constants

To raise our own errors, we need error numbers that do not conflict with those used by Visual Basic. The Visual Basic documentation says that error numbers in the range

$$vbObjectError \text{ to } vbObjectError + 65535$$

where *vbObjectError* is a built-in constant whose value is the signed integer -2147220991 (or &H80040000 as an unsigned hexadecimal integer), are designed to signal an error generated by an object. It further says that error numbers below *vbObjectError* + 512 may conflict with values reserved for

OLE, so these numbers are *verboten*. Thus, we are left with numbers in the range

$$vbObjectError + 512 \text{ to } vbObjectError + 65535$$

which should be plenty!

Many programmers like to assign constants to error numbers, since it tends to improve readability and cut down on the need for comments. Referring to the previous example, we could place the line

```
Public Const ErrBadDataCt = vbObjectError + 1024
```

in a standard module, for instance.

Handling the Error in the Calling Procedure

No matter how we decide to handle errors in the offending procedure, it is vitally important to fully and completely *document* the errors. In fact, the entire class module should be fully documented by describing its purpose, its input and output, and any possible errors.

This is important for in-procedure error handling, since often error messages are too cryptic to convey all the needed information to the user or to the debugging programmer. It is even more important to document errors that are passed up the calls list, because we may not be the one who writes the calling procedure, or we may need to write a calling procedure months or even years after writing the procedure that caused the error.

In fact, the method of handling an error that is passed from another procedure varies depending upon how that error is passed. If it is passed as the value of the function, for instance, then we will want code such as

```
ReturnValue = FunctionWithError()
If ReturnValue = ErrConstant1 then
   '' Deal with error 1
ElseIf ReturnValue = ErrConstant2 then
   '' Deal with error 2
End If
```

On the other hand, if an error is passed by raising (or reraising) the error, we can handle it either in the error-handler of the calling routine or on the spot, as in

```
On Error Resume Next
ReturnValue = FunctionWithError()
If Err.Number = ErrConstant1 then
    '' Deal with error 1
ElseIf ReturnValue = ErrConstant2 then
    '' Deal with error 2
End If
```

The *On Error Resume Next* line causes Visual Basic to execute the *If Err.Number* line even if the call to the function produces an error.

Clearly, we must rely on good documentation to help determine which course to take.

Errors Occurring in Events

It is important to realize that, when an error occurs in a Visual Basic *event* (as opposed to a user-defined procedure), the error cannot be passed up the calls list. It must be handled within the event.

To illustrate, start a new project and add the following code.

Snippet 2.1

To the *Form_Load* event, add the code

```
Private Sub Form_Load()

On Error GoTo ErrTest

' Create an object
Dim objT As Class1
Set objT = New Class1

' Call a method that generates an error
objT.AnError
```

```
Exit Sub

ErrTest:
MsgBox "From Form_Load: " & Err.Description
Exit Sub

End Sub
```

Insert a class module in the project and add the code

```
Private Sub Class_Initialize()
' Err.Raise Number:=vbObjectError + 512
End Sub

Public Sub AnError()
Err.Raise Number:=vbObjectError + 512
End Sub
```

This class has no properties or methods: Its sole purpose is to raise an error either when an object is initialized or when the *AnError* procedure is called.

Now run the project. You should get the error message *From Form_Load: OLE automation error"* indicating that the error in the subroutine *AnError* was passed to the calling routine. Now change the code by uncommenting the line that raises an error in the *Class_Initialize* event and run the program again. This time, you will get Visual Basic's error message dialog box, because the error in the *Initialize event* is not passed up the calls list.

Incidentally, the Visual Basic documentation says ". . . there is no procedure higher up the calls list than an event procedure . . . ." It is interesting to note that if you trace through the previous code snippet until you reach the *Initialize* event and check the calls list, you will find the *Form_Load* event at the top, followed by the entry <Non-Basic Code>, followed by the *Initialize* event.

An Error-Handling Example

To demonstrate the principles of error handling, let us consider an example, taken from the *CStudent* model of the previous chapter. As shown in Figure 2.1, code in the *CStudent* class calls a method in the *CReportCard* class.

Suppose the code that is called in the *CReportCard* class attempts to open a disk file to read a student's math grade, as follows:

```
Public Function GetMathGrade() As String

' Read a disk file to get math grade

Dim FName As String, SName as String
Dim FileExists As String
Dim MGrade as string

SName = InputBox("Enter student's full name. " & _
    "Leave blank to cancel.")

FName = InputBox("Enter complete path and " & _
    "filename of grade file.")

' Check for existence of file
FileExists = Dir(FName)

' Next comes code to:
' Open the file ...
' Read the file ...
' Return MGrade

End Function
```

The first step in designing error handling for this function is to make a list of the errors that we wish to treat. It may be acceptable in some cases to lump together some of the run-time errors under a single rubric. For instance, the message *Disk error* could be used to cover a multitude of sins, such as *Device unavailable*, *Disk not ready* and so on. Of course, the more condensing we do, the more difficult it will be for the user to determine how to rectify the error.

Visual Basic's Help system contains lists of trappable run-time errors, along with their error numbers. Consulting these lists will help avoid omissions. For the purposes of illustration, we will handle the run-time errors

- Error 53: File not found
- Error 71: Disk not ready

and the logical errors

- Grade missing or invalid
- Grade too low
- User did not enter grade file name

(The *Grade too low* error is for the benefit of my students, who don't like me to give failing grades.) Finally, we must not forget the ever-popular

- Unexpected error

which will cover the case of any run-time errors that we missed. In this case, the user will be informed that an error has occurred and will be given a description of the error but will not be given a chance to fix the error.

The next step is to decide, for each error, whether to handle it in the method that caused the error or to pass it to the calling procedure. For the sake of illustration, we handle all errors in the *GetMathGrade* function itself, except for *Grade too low*, which we will pass to the calling procedure.

Here are the constants for error handling. (The numbers 1024, 1025 and 1026 were chosen arbitrarily, from within the accepted range.)

```
Public Const ErrFileNotFound = 53
Public Const ErrDiskNotReady = 71
Public Const ErrGradeInvalid = vbObjectError + 1024
Public Const ErrGradeTooLow = vbObjectError + 1025
Public Const ErrBlankFileName = vbObjectError + 1026
```

In displaying error messages for logical errors, it is useful to display the error numbers as well, for use with the documentation. However, when Visual Basic displays an error number such as *vbObjectError* + 1024, it appears as a signed long integer, in this case, -214722048. This is not a very user-friendly error number, not to mention the fact that it looks like our program has so many potential errors that we had to resort to signed longs!

To deal with this issue, we can display the smaller numbers, such as 1024, 1025 and 1026, in any error messages, but with a qualification such as *MyApp Error 1024: Grade Invalid.* to distinguish the error from Visual Basic's error number 1024 (if it has one). Of course, we must also provide documentation to any *programmers* that might use our code, to the effect that the larger numbers (*vbObjectError* + 1024) are passed to calling procedures, as specified by Visual Basic, but the smaller numbers are displayed to end users. (If the documentation is for end users only, then documentation of the smaller numbers is sufficient, since they are not concerned with internal error handling.)

Here is *GetMathGrade* with error-handling code.

Snippet 2.2 — An Error-Handling Example

```
Public Function GetMathGrade() As String

' Read a disk file to get math grade

Dim FName As String, SName as String
Dim FileExists As String
Dim MGrade as string

' Enable error handling for run-time errors
On Error Goto ErrGetMathGrade

SName = InputBox("Enter student's full name. " & _
   "Leave blank to cancel.")

' Handle blank student
If Trim(SName) = "" then Exit Function

FName = InputBox("Enter complete path and " & _
   "filename of grade file.")

' Handle blank file name
If Trim(FName)="" then
   Err.Raise Number:= ErrBlankFileName
End If

' Check for existence of file
FileExists = Dir(FName)

' Next comes code to:
' Open the file ...
' Read the file ...
' Return MGrade ...

' Test code for tracing
' (as described in text to follow this listing)
'Open FName for Input as #1
'MGrade = "A"
```

```
'MGrade = "F"
'Mgrade = "Z"
' End Test Code

' Check for logical errors
If Instr("ABCDF",MGrade) = 0 then
   Err.Raise Number:=ErrGradeInvalid
End If
If MGrade = "F" then
   Err.Raise Number:=ErrGradeTooLow
End If

' Return grade
GetMathGrade = MGrade

Exit Function

' Error-handler
ErrGetMathGrade:

Select Case Err.Number

Case ErrBlankFileName
   If MsgBox ("To get math grade, enter name of " & _
      "grade file. Hit Cancel button to cancel.", _
      vbOKCancel) = vbCancel then

      Exit Function

   Else

      FName = InputBox("Enter complete path and " & _
         "filename of grade file.")
      ' Continue execution after Err.Raise line
      Resume Next

   End If

Case ErrGradeInvalid

   MsgBox "Error number " & _
      Err.Number-vbObjectError  & ": " _
      & "Grade is missing or invalid."
```

```
Case ErrGradeTooLow

  ' Reraise the error to pass it
  ' to calling procedure
  Err.Raise Number:=ErrGradeTooLow-vbObjectError, _
  Description := "But I do not deserve an F!", _
  Source := "GetMathGrade in CStudent."

Case ErrFileNotFound or ErrDiskNotReady

  MsgBox "Error number " & Err.Number & ": " _
  & Err.Description

Case Else

  MsgBox "Unexpected error in GetMathGrade. " & _
    "Please report error number " & Err.Number & _
    ". Error description: " & Err.Description & _
    " Source: " & Err.Source

End Select
Exit Function

End Function
```

To try out this code, key in the *GetMathGrade* function in the *CReport-Card* class, clear the *Form_Load* event in the main form of all existing code and key in the following:

```
Private Sub Form_Load()

On Error GoTo TestErr

Dim objStudent As Variant
Set objStudent = New CStudent

Dim objReportCard As CReportCard
Set objReportCard = New CReportCard

Set objStudent.ReportCard = objReportCard
```

```
objStudent.ReportCard.GetMathGrade

Exit Sub

' Error-handler
TestErr:
Select Case Err.Number

Case ErrGradeTooLow
   ' Documented error from another object
   MsgBox "Error " & Err.Number - vbObjectError & _
      ": " & Err.Description & " Source: " & _
      Err.Source

Case Is > vbObjectError and Is < vbObjectError+65536
   ' Unknown object errors
   MsgBox "Unknown Object Error " & Err.Number - _
   vbObjectError & ": " & Err.Description & _
   " Source: " & Err.Source

Case Else
   ' Other unknown errors
   MsgBox "Unknown Error " & Err.Number - _
   vbObjectError & ": " & Err.Description & _
   " Source: " & Err.Source

End Select

Exit Sub
End Sub
```

Now you can trace through the program. Try the following to test various error-handlers. (Enter any nonblank name for the student's name.)

- Trace the program. When you come to the request for a grade file name, just hit the *Enter* key without entering a file name. This should lead you into the *Case ErrBlankFileName* portion of the error-handling code.
- Uncomment the test code line *MGrade* = "Z" only in the code snippet and trace through the project. Enter any nonblank string for the grade file name. This should lead you to the *Case ErrGradeInvalid* portion of the error-handler.

- Uncomment the test code line *MGrade* = "F" only in the code snippet and trace through the project. Enter any nonblank string for the grade file name. This should lead you to the *Case ErrGradeTooLow* portion of the error handler. You will then be sent back to the *Form_Load* module to display the error message. The original error has been raised to the calling procedure!

- Make sure there is no floppy in the A drive and enter that drive letter in the grade file name input box. This should send you to the *Case ErrDiskNotReady* portion of the error-handler.

- Uncomment the test code line *Open FName...* only in the code snippet and trace the project. Put a floppy in the A drive and enter a nonexistent file name (e.g. a:\nofile) in the grade file name input box. This should send you to the *Case ErrFileNotFound* portion of the error-handler.

- Finally, uncomment the test code line *MGrade* = "A" only in the code snippet and trace through the project. It should run without error.

Note that we have included a *Select Case* construct in the error-handling routine of the above *Form_Load* event. The first case handles the *documented* error from the *CStudent* class module. The second case handles unknown object errors (indicated by the range of the error number). These may be unexpected, and perhaps even undocumented, errors passed to us from further down the calls list or they may be errors generated within the current module. The final case catches other unknown errors.

There is one source of errors that we did not deal with directly (but is included in the *Case Else* statement). If our program uses OLE automation objects from another application, it is possible that an unhandled error may occur in that application. If the application was written in Visual Basic, it will return a proper error to our program. (More on this in the chapter on OLE automation.) But if the application sending the unhandled error is not a Visual Basic application, then Visual Basic will automatically remap the error to error number 440: *OLE automation error*. The Visual Basic documentation says that if we decide to pass this error on, it should be done with a new error number, of our own choosing.

Chapter 3
Turing Machines — A Simple Object-Oriented Application

In this chapter, we present a simple but complete example of an application that is programmed in an object-oriented style. The example is that of a *Turing machine*, which, simply put, is a model of a computer. You need have no prior knowledge of Turing machines to read this chapter, since we will take a moment now to discuss what you need to know, beginning with a bit of background. Also, since this material will not be used later, you may skip this chapter if you wish.

The complete source code for this application should be available on the Springer-Verlag Web site, under

http://www.springer-ny.com/supplements/sroman

What Is an Algorithm?

Ever since the 1930s, computer scientists have been trying to figure out just what kinds of problems a "computer" can solve. This leads to the notion of an *algorithm*. Intuitively speaking, an algorithm is just a set of simple instructions or rules for attempting to answer a given question or perform a given operation. These instructions must be so *idiot-proof* that even a machine, which cannot do anything original or creative, can carry them out.

Also, an algorithm must be guaranteed to produce an output, from a given *valid* input, after a finite amount of time. On the other hand, given an *invalid* input, an algorithm may compute forever. For instance, an algorithm that computes the square root of a perfect square, such as 9, 16, 25 or 36, does not need to stop if applied to a number that is not a perfect square.

The problem with the previous definition of algorithm is that it is too informal. In general, we can never hope to show that an algorithm does *not* exist for a particular problem unless we have a *precise*, formal definition of algorithm.

Over the past 60 years, there have been many proposals for a precise definition of the term algorithm. They have mostly taken the form of designing a model of an "ideal" computer and arguing that a procedure is an algorithm if and only if it can be carried out by that model of a computer. Note that we cannot use a real computer, such as a PC, for this, because real computers are limited in resources and we do not want to put an upper limit on how long an algorithm can take to perform its function (only that it must stop eventually).

Just to give you an idea of the effort that has gone into this endeavor, here is a list of the types of models that have been considered. (Most of these models describe the types of *functions* that can be computed by the model.) Don't worry if these names make no sense to you; this list is just for effect, so to speak.

- Gödel-Herbrand-Kleene (1936) — General recursive functions
- Church (1936) — Lambda-definable functions
- Gödel-Kleene (1936) — Partial-recursive functions
- Turing (1936) — Functions computable by Turing machines
- Post (1943) — Functions defined from canonical deduction systems
- Markov (1951) — Functions given by a certain procedure over a finite alphabet
- Shepherdson-Sturgis (1963) — Unlimited register machines

This is quite an impressive list of models for the notion of algorithm. It is also quite diverse. Many of these models seem, at first, to bear no relationship with the other models. However — and here comes the punch line — *each of the above proposals for the characterization of algorithm leads to exactly the same result*! In other words, if a function can be computed by one of these methods, it can be computed by all of these methods.

This brings us to the famous *Church's Thesis*, accepted by most computer scientists. Church's Thesis says that, in view of the above strong (perhaps overwhelming) evidence, we should *formally* define the term algorithm by saying that a procedure *is* an algorithm if and only if it can be implemented on any one (and hence all) of the above computer models. Let us emphasize that Church's Thesis is not subject to proof — it is more in the nature of a definition based on many decades of observation.

What Is a Turing Machine?

The most famous model of a computer is the Turing machine, named after the brilliant mathematician Alan Turing, who first described his machine in 1936. There are many equivalent descriptions of these machines. We will simply pick one and content ourselves with an informal definition.

Informal Definition of a Turing Machine

Simply put, a Turing machine is a machine with a tape and a read/write head, as pictured in Figure 3.1. The read/write head reads from and writes to the cells of the tape and moves along the tape, according to a set of instructions that are part of the machine. Initially, symbols are placed in some of the cells of the tape, starting at the far left cell, the head is moved to the far left cell, and the power is turned on. The instructions are followed until the machine stops. The final contents of the tape are considered the output of the machine.

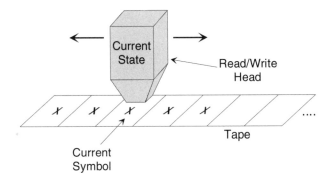

Figure 3.1

Figure 3.2 shows our visual interface for a Turing machine. To simplify the coding, we have implemented the read/write head as a long text box that sits below the tape. The current position of the head is denoted by changing the current cell to a color that matches the color of the read/write head. (In Figure 3.2, the head is positioned over the leftmost cell.) The controls below the horizontal line in Figure 3.2 exist simply to help us control the machine and observe its current status. They are not part of the Turing machine proper.

Now let us fill in the details of the description of a Turing machine.

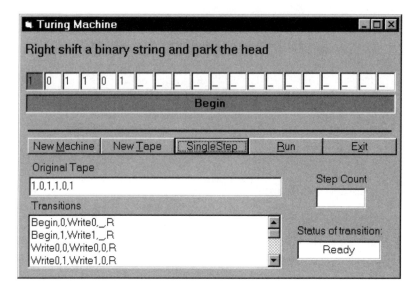

Figure 3.2

Tape

As mentioned, a Turing machine has a *tape* that is divided into cells. The first cell is the leftmost cell, but the tape can stretch as far to the right as necessary. There is also a finite set of symbols called the *tape alphabet*. Each cell may contain a single symbol from that alphabet.

Read/Write Head

A Turing machine has a *read/write head*, which is always positioned over one of the cells of the tape. That cell is called the *current cell*. The symbol in the current cell is called the *current symbol*. When the head is under the leftmost cell, it is said to be *parked*.

States

At all times, a Turing machine is in one of a finite number of possible *states*, denoted by the word in the text box representing the read/write head. (The machine in Figure 3.2 is in the state called *Begin*.) One of the states is designated as the *initial state* and one is designated as the *final state*.

Input Alphabet

To begin a Turing machine computation, the operator places some symbols from the tape alphabet in the leftmost cells of the tape (this is the input), parks the head and sets the machine to its initial state. Actually, the initial symbols often are restricted to a *subset* of the tape alphabet known as the *input alphabet*. For instance, even though we may allow the tape symbols 0, 1 and _ (where the underscore denotes a blank cell), we may want to restrict the *initial* input to just the binary digits 0 and 1 (no blanks initially).

Machine Computations

Instructions for the machine have the form

> CurrentState, CurrentSymbol → NewState, NewSymbol, Direction

and are called *transitions*, or *single-step computations*. For instance, the transition

$$\textit{Begin},1 \rightarrow \textit{State2},0,\text{Right}$$

is interpreted as: If the current state is *Begin* and the current symbol is a 1, then change to state *State2*, write a 0 in the current cell and move the head one cell to the right.

   More specifically, a single-step computation of the machine consists of taking the following actions. Based on the current symbol and the current state of the machine, do the following:

1. Enter a new state (perhaps the same as the previous state).
2. Write a symbol from the tape alphabet to the current cell.
3. Move the head left one cell (if it is not at the leftmost position), or right one cell, or do not move the head.

   It is customary to speak in terms of the *transition function* T of a Turing machine, which is just the function T defined by

$$\text{T}(\textit{CurrentState}, \textit{CurrentSymbol}) = (\textit{NewState}, \textit{NewSymbol}, \textit{Direction})$$

The function T is actually referred to as a *partial* function, because it need not be defined on all pairs (*CurrentState*, *CurrentSymbol*).

A *complete computation* consists of repeating single-step computations until the machine enters its final state (if it ever does). The symbols on the tape then represent the *output* of the machine.

Illegal Moves

If a Turing machine attempts to move left while the head is parked, we say that an *inadmissible* move has occurred. Turing machines must be designed to avoid inadmissible moves. (Think of these as bugs.) Note that the list of possible single-step computations need not cover all possibilities. There may be no description of what to do if the machine gets into a certain state with a certain current symbol. In this case, the machine is in an *undefined state*, a condition also to be avoided.

Describing a Turing Machine

We will use an ordinary text file to describe a Turing machine. Our example is a very simple machine that takes a binary string as input, shifts that input one position to the right on the tape and then parks the head over a blank cell. Thus, the input alphabet is {0,1} and the tape alphabet is {0,1,_}, where the underscore denotes a blank.

The text file for our example is given below. Note that the expression for the transition function T is written (on one line) as

```
Transition=CurrentState,CurrentSymbol,NewState,
    NewSymbol,Direction
```

in the text file.

```
; ***Purpose of the machine***
; A Turing Machine to right-shift a binary string
; and park the head.

; ***Description for top of form***
Description=Right shift a binary string and park the
head

; ***Tape Alphabet***
; Use an underscore for a blank symbol.
; Prefix * to symbols NOT in the input alphabet.
Alphabet=0,1,*_
```

```
; ***Possible States of the Machine***
; Prefix (I) to initial state and
; (F) to final state.
States=(I)Begin,Write0,Write1,Parking,(F)Done

; ***Transitions***
Transition=Begin,0,Write0,_,R
Transition=Begin,1,Write1,_,R

Transition=Write0,0,Write0,0,R
Transition=Write0,1,Write1,0,R
Transition=Write0,_,Parking,0,L

Transition=Write1,0,Write0,1,R
Transition=Write1,1,Write1,1,R
Transition=Write1,_,Parking,1,L

Transition=Parking,0,Parking,0,L
Transition=Parking,1,Parking,1,L
Transition=Parking,_,Done,_,N
```

Note that we use a descriptive word for each possible state of the machine. The states describe what the machine needs to do next. Here is a description of the actions of the machine. Refer to the file contents as you read.

- In the initial state *Begin*, read the current symbol. Enter the state *Write0* if the current symbol is a 0 and state *Write1* if the current symbol is a 1. In this way, the state of the machine records the contents of the first cell and knows what to do on the next computation. Then write a blank to the cell and move the head right.

- The machine is now in state *Write0* or *Write1*. While reading the rest of the input string, the machine will switch between these two states according to what it reads in the current cell (read a 0, switch to state *Write0*; read a 1, switch to state *Write1*), then write a symbol according to its state (before switching states, that is), and then move right. This continues until a blank is encountered. Thus, for instance, if the current state is *Write0* and the current symbol is a 1, the machine should write a 0, go into state *Write1* and move right one cell.

- When the machine reads a blank, it writes as before (according to its state) but then enters the state *Parking*, indicating that, from then on, it should move left until it encounters the leftmost cell in the tape, which is the only blank cell to the left of the head. (There is no intrinsic way for a machine to know that it is parked. The machine's designer must program this into the state or the current symbol.)

Coding a Turing Machine

The first step in coding our Turing machine is to decide what objects (that is, what classes) are appropriate for the project and how these objects should be related. The object hierarchy is shown in Figure 3.3, where the collection classes are indicated by trapezoidal boxes.

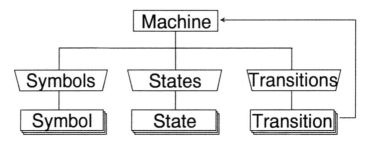

Figure 3.3. The object hierarchy

Here is a brief description of the purpose of each class.

Objects of the *Symbol* class are the "letters" in the tape alphabet. The *Symbols* collection class will hold these letters (gotten by reading the machine file) and thus constitutes the tape alphabet of the machine. Each *Symbol* object has a name property and a Boolean property that signals whether or not it is in the input alphabet. The *Symbols* class also has a Boolean method that determines whether a given string is a symbol in the tape alphabet. This will be used in validating a transition, to make sure it uses only valid tape symbols.

Objects in the *State* class are the possible states of the machine. These objects need only a name property. The *States* class is a collection class holding the *State* objects and has a single Boolean method to determine whether a given string is a state of the machine. This will also be used to validate the transitions in the machine file.

Objects in the *Transition* class are intended to describe the application of the transition function on a single input pair (*CurrentState, CurrentSymbol*). Thus, an object represents a 5-tuple

(*CurrentState, CurrentSymbol, NewState, NewSymbol, Direction*)

We implement this simply by defining five properties for a *Transition* object — the five properties in the 5-tuple above.

Validation in the *Transition* class presents us with a bit of a dilemma. The issue is that, when attempting to add a new transition (from the machine file) to the *Transitions* collection class, we need to verify that *CurrentState* and *NewState* are valid members of the *States* collection, and similarly for *CurrentSymbol* and *CurrentState*. But this validation requires use of the external collection classes *Symbols* and *States*, raising the question of how the *Transition* class should get access to these collection classes.

There are several possibilities. First, note that a running Turing machine application will have a single *Machine* object, a single *Symbols* collection object and a single *States* collection object. Now, one possibility is to add two additional properties to the *Transition* class; namely, *Symbols* and *States*. These properties would be set to refer to the aforementioned collection objects, as shown in Figure 3.4, thus giving *Transition* objects the required access to the collections. The object hierarchy for this design is pictured in Figure 3.4.

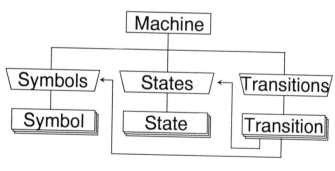

Figure 3.4

An alternative is to add a single property to the *Transition* class, called *Machine*, which, of course, refers to the *Machine* object. Then the *Transition* class will have access to the *Symbols* and *States* collections, by way of the *Machine* object. This does create a circular reference and so care must be exercised in releasing objects. We opt for this approach, as indicated by the arrow on the far right of Figure 3.3.

The *Machine* class represents the machine. As the object hierarchy indicates, the *Machine* object has three object properties (the three collection classes). Put another way, the *Machine* object *contains* a *Symbols* collection, a *States* collection and a *Transitions* collection.

It also has a variety of other properties:

- *Description* (describes the purpose of the machine)
- *Current State*
- *Initial State*
- *Final State*
- *Current Cell*
- *Tape* (an array holding the tape contents)
- *MachineStatus* (Machine file is *Loaded* or *Unloaded*)
- *TapeStatus* (*Loaded*, *Unloaded* or *OutOfTape*)

The *CMachine* class has three methods:

- *ReadMachineFile*, to read (load) a new machine file
- *NewTape*, to get (load) a new tape from the user
- *SingleStep*, to perform a single-step computation

A *Run* method is not needed, since that can be handled by whoever is using the *Machine* object, by repeated calls to the *SingleStep* method.

Error Handling

Let us now turn to error handling. Run-time errors should be minimal. However, since the machine description file must be opened, we need to deal with a host of potential disk-related errors, such as *Disk not ready*, *Device unavailable* and so on.

Logical errors present a more complicated picture. Here are the possibilities, together with the location in which each might arise.

Symbol Class:
　　Blank symbol name in machine file

Symbols Collection Class *Add* method:
　　Duplicate symbol name in machine file

State Class:
　　Blank state name in machine file

States Collection Class *Add* method:
　　Duplicate state name in machine file

Transition Class:
　　Invalid state in transition in machine file
　　Invalid symbol in transition in machine file
　　Invalid direction in transition in machine file

Transitions Collection Class *Add* method:
　　Duplicate transition in machine file

Machine Class:
　　In *ReadMachineFile*:
　　　　Machine file not found
　　　　No alphabet in machine file
　　　　No state in machine file
　　　　No transitions in machine file
　　In *NewTape*:
　　　　No machine loaded
　　　　User provided invalid tape symbol
　　In *SingleStep*:
　　　　No tape loaded
　　　　Inadmissible transition
　　　　Undefined transition
　　　　Out of tape

　　Most of the errors stem from a problem in the machine file and will require that the user fix the machine file and start again. In these cases, the calling routine is *ReadMachineFile*, and so our strategy will be to pass these errors to the *ReadMachineFile* method for handling. The *ReadMachineFile* method will inform the user that there is an error in the machine file, describe the nature of the error and then set the *MachineStatus* property to *Unloaded*, so no further action can be taken until the user loads another machine file.

Now let us take a closer look at the individual classes and how they are actually coded.

The Symbol Class

Starting at the bottom of the hierarchy, the objects of the Symbol class *CSymbol* are the symbols in the tape alphabet. Note that these symbols may be strings of any length. A *CSymbol* object has two properties: *Name*, which is the name of the symbol (for example, 0, 1, A, B, 1x or Fred); and *InputSymbol*, which is a Boolean value indicating whether or not the symbol belongs to the input alphabet of the machine. Here is the code for the *CSymbol* class:

```
' The Symbol Class
' Properties: Name, InputSymbol (Boolean)

Private mName As String

Public InputSymbol As Boolean

Public Property Get Name() As String
Name = mName
End Property

Public Property Let Name(pName As String)
' No blank names
If Trim(pName) <> "" Then
    mName = pName
Else
    Err.Raise Number:=ERR_BLANK_SYMBOL
End If
End Property
```

The Symbols Collection Class

The collection class *CSymbols* holds the *CSymbol* objects; that is, it holds the tape alphabet of the machine. Since the *Name* property must be unique, we can use it as the collection key. The *CSymbols* class has a Boolean method called *IsSymbol* that determines whether or not its input is a valid symbol. This method is used by the *CTransitions* collection to validate a (potential) *Transition* object before adding it to the collection.

```vb
' The Symbols Collection Class
' Property: Count
' Methods: Add, Item, IsSymbol

Private mSymbols As New Collection

Public Property Get Count() As Long
Count = mSymbols.Count
End Property

Public Function Item(vKey As Variant) As CSymbol
Set Item = mSymbols.Item(vKey)
End Function

Public Function Add(Name As String, InputSymbol As _
  Boolean) As CSymbol

' Instance a new CSymbol object
' to use in adding to collection
Dim lSymbol As New CSymbol

' Enable error handling to catch
' duplicate state names
On Error GoTo ErrAddSymbols

With lSymbol
    ' Set properties
    .Name = Name
    .InputSymbol = InputSymbol
    ' Add to collection, using unique Name as key
    mSymbols.Add lSymbol, lSymbol.Name
End With

' Return the object added
Set Add = lSymbol

Exit Function
ErrAddSymbols:
    Select Case Err.Number
        Case ERR_DUP_KEY
            ' Make error more specific
            Err.Raise Number:=ERR_DUP_SYMBOL
```

```
            Case ERR_BLANK_SYMBOL
                ' Send it up
                Err.Raise Number:=ERR_BLANK_SYMBOL
            Case Else
                ' Any other error
                Err.Raise Number:=ERR_UNKNOWN_ERROR
        End Select
        Exit Function

End Function

Public Function IsSymbol(pName As String) As Boolean

' Returns True if pSymbol is a Symbol

Dim lSymbol As New CSymbol

IsSymbol = False
For Each lSymbol In mSymbols
    If pName = lSymbol.Name Then
        IsSymbol = True
        Exit For
    End If
Next lSymbol

End Function
```

The State Class

The objects of the class *CState* are the possible states of the machine. State objects have only a *Name* property.

```
' The State Class
' Property: Name

Private mName As String

Public Property Get Name() As String
Name = mName
End Property

Public Property Let Name(pName As String)
```

```
' No blank names
If Trim(pName) <> "" Then
    mName = pName
Else
    Err.Raise Number:=ERR_BLANK_STATE
End If
End Property
```

The States Collection Class

The collection class *CStates* holds the *CState* objects. Hence, it is the collection of all possible states of the machine. Since the *Name* property must be unique, we can use it as the collection key. The *CStates* class has a Boolean method called *IsState* that determines whether or not its input is a valid state. This method is used by the *CTransitions* collection to validate a (potential) *Transition* object before adding it to the collection.

```
' The States Collection Class
' Property: Count
' Methods: Add, Item, IsState(Boolean)

Private mStates As New Collection

Public Property Get Count() As Long
Count = mStates.Count
End Property

Public Function Item(vKey As Variant) As CState
Set Item = mStates.Item(vKey)
End Function

Public Function Add(Name As String) As CState

' Instance a new CState object
Dim lState As New CState

' Enable error handling to catch
' duplicate state names
On Error GoTo ErrAddStates

With lState
    ' Set property
```

```
            .Name = Name
            ' Add to collection, using name as key
            mStates.Add lState, lState.Name
    End With

    ' Return the object added
    Set Add = lState

    Exit Function
ErrAddStates:
    Select Case Err.Number
        Case ERR_DUP_KEY
            ' Make error more specific
            Err.Raise Number:=ERR_DUP_STATE
        Case ERR_BLANK_STATE
            ' Send it up
            Err.Raise Number:=ERR_BLANK_STATE
        Case Else
            ' Any other error
            Err.Raise Number:=ERR_UNKNOWN_ERROR
    End Select
    Exit Function
End Function

Public Function IsState(pName As String) As Boolean

    ' Returns True if pState is a State
    Dim lState As New CState

    IsState = False
    For Each lState In mStates
        If pName = lState.Name Then
            IsState = True
            Exit For
        End If
    Next lState

End Function
```

The Transition Class

The *Transition* class objects represent possible transitions of the machine. Each has five properties: *CurrentState*, *CurrentSymbol*, *NewState*, *NewSymbol* and *Direction*. The *Transition* class needs no methods. As mentioned before, validation of the states and symbols is done through the *IsState* and *IsSymbol* methods of the respective collection classes. For instance, to validate a potential state, we use

```
If mMachine.States.IsState(pCurState) Then ...
```

which executes the *IsState* method of the *States* collection object contained in the *Machine* object.

```
' The Transition Class
'   A transition is:
'   CurState,CurSymbol,NewState,NewSymbol,Direction
' Methods: None

' Properties
Private mCurState As String
Private mCurSymbol As String
Private mNewState As String
Private mNewSymbol As String
Private mDirection As String
Private mMachine As CMachine

Public Property Get Machine() As CMachine
Set Machine = mMachine
End Property

Public Property Set Machine(pMachine As CMachine)
Set mMachine = pMachine
End Property

Public Property Let CurState(pCurState As String)
' Validate pCurState as a state
If mMachine.States.IsState(pCurState) Then
    mCurState = pCurState
Else
    Err.Raise Number:=ERR_INVALID_STATE
End If
```

```
End Property

Public Property Get CurState() As String
CurState = mCurState
End Property

Public Property Let CurSymbol(pCurSymbol As String)
' Validate pCurSymbol as a symbol
If mMachine.Symbols.IsSymbol(pCurSymbol) Then
    mCurSymbol = pCurSymbol
Else
    Err.Raise Number:=ERR_INVALID_SYMBOL
End If
End Property

Public Property Get CurSymbol() As String
CurSymbol = mCurSymbol
End Property

Public Property Let NewState(pNewState As String)
' Validate pNewState as a state
If mMachine.States.IsState(pNewState) Then
    mNewState = pNewState
Else
    Err.Raise Number:=ERR_INVALID_STATE
End If
End Property

Public Property Get NewState() As String
NewState = mNewState
End Property

Public Property Let NewSymbol(pNewSymbol As String)
' Validate pNewSymbol as a symbol
If mMachine.Symbols.IsSymbol(pNewSymbol) Then
    mNewSymbol = pNewSymbol
Else
    Err.Raise Number:=ERR_INVALID_SYMBOL
End If
End Property

Public Property Get NewSymbol() As String
NewSymbol = mNewSymbol
```

```
End Property

Public Property Let Direction(pDir As String)
' Validate pDir as "R", "L" or "N"
pDir = UCase$(Left$(pDir, 1))
If InStr("LRN", pDir) Then
    mDirection = pDir
Else
    Err.Raise Number:=ERR_INVALID_DIR
End If
End Property

Public Property Get Direction() As String
Direction = mDirection
End Property
```

The Transitions Collection Class

The *CTransitions* collection class holds the individual *CTransition* objects and thus makes up the *transition function* for the machine.

The key for this collection is a combination of *CurState* and *CurSymbol*, since the transition function has at most one line with the same (*CurState,CurSymbol*) pair. Otherwise, it wouldn't be a function!

The class has a method called *Transition* that applies the transition function. In particular, for an input (*CurState, CurSymbol*), we would like the output (*NewState, NewSymbol, Direction*), along with an indication of the success of the function; say in the form of a string whose value is "Undefined" if the transition function is not defined for this input and "Admissible" otherwise.

To accommodate all of this output, we use additional parameters that are called by reference. Hence, the *Transition* function is declared as follows:

```
Public Function Transition(ByVal pCurState As _
String, ByVal pCurSymbol As String, _
ByRef pNewState As String, ByRef pNewSymbol As _
String, ByRef pDirection As String) As String
```

After this function is called, we check for a return value of "Admissible." If this is the return value, we then read the parameters passed by reference to get the values of *NewState, NewSymbol* and *Direction*. Here is the code for the *Transitions* class:

```
' Transitions Collection Class
'
' Property: Count
' Methods:
'    Add, Item
'    Transition (applies the transition function)

Private mTransitions As New Collection

Public Property Get Count() As Long
Count = mTransitions.Count
End Property

Public Function Item(vKey As Variant) As CTransition
Set Item = mTransitions.Item(vKey)
End Function

Public Function Transition(ByVal pCurState As _
String, ByVal pCurSymbol As String, _
ByRef pNewState As String, ByRef pNewSymbol As _
String, ByRef pDirection As String) As String

' Returns "Undefined" if transition function not
' defined for this (state,symbol) pair and returns
' "Admissible" otherwise
' Also returns the values of NewState, NewSymbol
' and Direction

Dim RetValue As String
Dim vTrans As Variant

RetValue = "Undefined"
For Each vTrans In mTransitions

    If pCurState = vTrans.CurState _
      And pCurSymbol = vTrans.CurSymbol Then

        RetValue = "Admissible"
        pNewState = vTrans.NewState
        pNewSymbol = vTrans.NewSymbol
        pDirection = vTrans.Direction
        Exit For
```

```
    End If

Next vTrans

Transition = RetValue

End Function

Public Function Add(Machine As CMachine, CurState _
As String, CurSymbol As String, NewState As _
String, NewSymbol As String, Direction As String) _
As CTransition

' Define a new CTransition instance
' to use in adding to collection
Dim lTransition As New CTransition

On Error GoTo ErrAddTrans

With lTransition
    ' Set properties - Machine property first!
    Set .Machine = Machine
    .CurState = CurState
    .CurSymbol = CurSymbol
    .NewState = NewState
    .NewSymbol = NewSymbol
    .Direction = Direction
    ' ID is a unique combination of CurState and
    ' CurSymbol
    ' Add to collection
    mTransitions.Add lTransition, CurState & "/" &
CurSymbol
End With
' Return the object added
Set Add = lTransition

Exit Function

ErrAddTrans:
    Select Case Err.Number
        Case ERR_DUP_KEY
            ' Make error more specific
            Err.Raise Number:=ERR_DUP_TRANS
```

```
      Case ERR_INVALID_STATE
          ' Send it up
          Err.Raise Number:=ERR_INVALID_STATE
      Case ERR_INVALID_SYMBOL
          ' Send it up
          Err.Raise Number:=ERR_INVALID_SYMBOL
      Case ERR_INVALID_DIR
          ' Send it up
          Err.Raise Number:=ERR_INVALID_DIR
      Case Else
          ' Any other error
          Err.Raise Number:=ERR_UNKNOWN_ERROR
      End Select
   Exit Function

End Function
```

The Machine Class

The *CMachine* class does the heavy work. The methods of this class are *ReadMachineFile*, *NewTape* and *SingleStep*. It has several ordinary properties describing the status of the machine: *Description, CurrentState, InitialState, FinalState, CurrentCell, Tape, MachineStatus, TapeStatus*. It also has three object properties: *Symbols, States* and *Transitions*, the latter being of type *CTransitions*. Hence, a *CMachine* object contains a *CTransitions* transition function object.

We have implemented the machine's tape as an array by declaring

```
Private mTapeArray(1 To TapeLen) As String
```

However, a property cannot be of type *Array*. One way around this is to store the array in a property of type *Variant*, as in the *Property Get* procedure shown below. We may still refer to individual components of the array using the syntax *Tape*(i).

```
Public Property Get Tape() As Variant
' Tape property is a variant containing mTapeArray
Tape = mTapeArray
End Property
```

The methods of the *CMachine* class are pretty straightforward. The *New-Machine* method takes the machine file name as parameter, checks for the existence of that file and raises an error if no such file exists. If the file exists, it opens that file and reads in the tape alphabet, the set of states, the initial and final states and the machine's description. It also reads the transitions and fills the *CTransitions* collection. Finally, it sets the *MachineStatus* property to "Loaded."

The *NewTape* method asks the user for a new tape. If the tape is invalid, an error message is issued; otherwise, it fills the tape array and sets the *TapeStatus* property to "Loaded."

The *SingleStep* method applies the transition function to the current (*state,symbol*) pair, by calling the *Transition* method of the *CTransitions* collection class, as follows:

```
RetValue = mTransitions.Transition(mCurState, _
mTapeArray(mCurCell), pNewSt, pNewSym, pDir)
```

If the return value is not "Undefined," then we know that the function was successful and we can set the new values of the state of the machine and the current symbol and move the read/write head. The *SingleStep* method returns one of the strings *NoMachine, NoTape, Inadmissible, Undefined, OffTheTape* or *Admissible* to indicate the results of the single-step computation. (The value *OffTheTape* would not occur on a real Turing machine, but any computer model of a Turing machine must necessarily be finite.)

Here is the code.

```
' The Machine Class
'
' Methods: ReadMachineFile, NewTape, SingleStep
'
' General properties
Private mDescription As String
Private mCurState As String
Private mInitialState As String
Private mFinalState As String
Private mCurCell As Integer
Private mTapeArray(1 To TapeLen) As String

' Reporting properties
Private mMachineStatus As String  '= Loaded, Unloaded
Private mTapeStatus As String     '= Loaded, Unloaded
```

```vb
' Object properties
Private mSymbols As CSymbols
Private mStates As CStates
Private mTransitions As CTransitions

Public Property Get TapeStatus() As String
TapeStatus = mTapeStatus
End Property

Public Property Get MachineStatus() As String
MachineStatus = mMachineStatus
End Property

Public Property Get Description() As String
Description = mDescription
End Property

Public Property Get InitialState() As String
InitialState = mInitialState
End Property

Public Property Get FinalState() As String
FinalState = mFinalState
End Property

Public Property Get CurState() As String
CurState = mCurState
End Property

Public Property Get CurCell() As Integer
CurCell = mCurCell
End Property

Public Property Get Symbols() As CSymbols
Set Symbols = mSymbols
End Property

Public Property Get States() As CStates
Set States = mStates
End Property

Public Property Get Transitions() As CTransitions
```

```vb
Set Transitions = mTransitions
End Property

Public Property Set Transitions(pTransitions As
CTransitions)
' Needed to break circular references
Set mTransitions = pTransitions
End Property

Public Property Get Tape() As Variant
' Tape property is a variant containing mTapeArray
Tape = mTapeArray
End Property

Public Sub ReadMachineFile(pMachineFile As String)

' Check for existence of machine file
' Instance and fill new States collection
' Instance and fill new Symbols collection
' Instance and fill new CTransitions collection
' Handles error messages

Dim Fr As Integer, SafetyCt As Integer
Dim x As Integer, i As Integer, y As Integer
Dim sLine As String, sTmp As String
Dim lCurState As String, lCurSymbol As String
Dim lNewState As String, lNewSymbol As String
Dim lDirection As String

On Error GoTo ErrCMachine

mMachineStatus = "Unloaded"

' Check for machine file and open it
If Dir$(pMachineFile) = "" Then
    Err.Raise ERR_MACHINE_NOT_FOUND
Else
    Fr = FreeFile
    Open pMachineFile For Input As #Fr
End If

' New collection objects
Set mSymbols = New CSymbols
```

```
Set mStates = New CStates

Do While Not EOF(Fr)

    Line Input #Fr, sLine

    ' Parse Alphabet= line
    If LCase$(Left$(sLine, 9)) = "alphabet=" Then
        sLine = Mid$(sLine, 10) & ","
        SafetyCt = 0
        x = InStr(sLine, ",")
        Do While x > 0 And SafetyCt < MaxSymbolsCt
            SafetyCt = SafetyCt + 1
            ' Get candidate
            sTmp = Trim$(Left$(sLine, x - 1))
            ' Check for member of input alphabet
            If Left$(sTmp, 1) <> "*" Then
                mSymbols.Add sTmp, True
            Else
                sTmp = Mid$(sTmp, 2)
                mSymbols.Add sTmp, False
            End If
            ' Strip off candidate
            sLine = Mid$(sLine, x + 1)
            x = InStr(sLine, ",")
        Loop
    End If

    ' Parse States= line
    If LCase$(Left$(sLine, 7)) = "states=" Then
        sLine = Mid$(sLine, 8) & ","
        SafetyCt = 0
        x = InStr(sLine, ",")
        Do While x > 0 And SafetyCt < MaxStateCt
            SafetyCt = SafetyCt + 1
            sTmp = Trim$(Left$(sLine, x - 1))
            ' Check for initial/final states
            If Left$(sTmp, 3) = "(I)" Then
                sTmp = Mid$(sTmp, 4)
                mInitialState = sTmp
            ElseIf Left$(sTmp, 3) = "(F)" Then
                sTmp = Mid$(sTmp, 4)
                mFinalState = sTmp
```

```
                End If
                mStates.Add sTmp
                sLine = Mid$(sLine, x + 1)
                x = InStr(sLine, ",")
            Loop
            Exit Do
        End If

        ' Description= line
        If LCase$(Left$(sLine, 12)) = "description=" _
            Then
                ' Max 50 characters
                mDescription = Mid$(sLine, 13, 50)
        End If

Loop
Close #Fr

' Take care of bad Alphabet/States
If mSymbols.Count = 0 Then
    Err.Raise ERR_NO_ALPHABET
ElseIf mStates.Count = 0 Then
    Err.Raise ERR_NO_STATES
End If

' Set current cell and state
mCurCell = 1
mCurState = mInitialState

' Now do Transition function
Set mTransitions = New CTransitions
' Reopen machine file
Fr = FreeFile
Open pMachineFile For Input As #Fr

Do While Not EOF(Fr)

    Line Input #Fr, sLine

    If LCase$(Left$(sLine, 11)) = "transition=" Then
        sLine = Mid$(sLine, 12) & ","
        x = InStr(sLine, ",")
```

```
            If x > 0 Then lCurState = _
               Trim$(Left$(sLine, x - 1))

            y = x + 1: x = InStr(y, sLine, ",")

            If x > y Then lCurSymbol = _
               Trim$(Mid$(sLine, y, x - y))

            y = x + 1: x = InStr(x + 1, sLine, ",")

            If x > y Then lNewState = _
               Trim$(Mid$(sLine, y, x - y))

            y = x + 1: x = InStr(x + 1, sLine, ",")

            If x > y Then lNewSymbol = _
               Trim$(Mid$(sLine, y, x - y))

            y = x + 1: x = InStr(x + 1, sLine, ",")

            If x > y Then lDirection = _
               Trim$(Mid$(sLine, y, x - y))

            mTransitions.Add Machine:=Me, _
                        CurState:=lCurState, _
                        CurSymbol:=lCurSymbol, _
                        NewState:=lNewState, _
                        NewSymbol:=lNewSymbol, _
                        Direction:=lDirection
      End If

ReadNext:
Loop
Close #Fr
' Take care of no transitions
If mTransitions.Count = 0 Then
     Err.Raise ERR_NO_TRANS
End If

mMachineStatus = "Loaded"

Exit Sub
```

```
' Error-Handler
ErrCMachine:
    mMachineStatus = "Unloaded"

    ' Note: These messages are a bit cryptic to save
    ' space

    Select Case Err.Number
        Case ERR_MACHINE_NOT_FOUND
            MsgBox "Could not find machine file.", _
            vbCritical
        Case ERR_NO_ALPHABET
            MsgBox "Could not find 'Alphabet=' " & _
            "line or line empty.", vbCritical
        Case ERR_NO_STATES
            MsgBox "Could not find 'States=' " & _
            "line or line empty.", vbCritical
        Case ERR_NO_TRANS
            MsgBox "No transitions in machine " & _
            "file.", vbCritical
        Case ERR_BLANK_STATE
            MsgBox "Blank state names not " & _
            "allowed in machine file.", vbCritical
        Case ERR_BLANK_SYMBOL
            MsgBox "Blank symbol names not " & _
            "allowed in machine file.", vbCritical
        Case ERR_DUP_STATE
            MsgBox "Duplicate state in machine " & _
            "file.", vbCritical
        Case ERR_DUP_SYMBOL
            MsgBox "Duplicate symbol in " & _
            "machine file.", vbCritical
        Case ERR_INVALID_STATE
            MsgBox "Invalid state in transition.", _
            vbCritical
        Case ERR_INVALID_SYMBOL
            MsgBox "Invalid symbol in transition.",_
            vbCritical
        Case ERR_INVALID_DIR
            MsgBox "Invalid direction in " & _
            "transition.", vbCritical
        Case ERR_DUP_TRANS
            MsgBox "Duplicate transition in " & _
```

```
                        "machine file.", vbCritical
              Case ERR_UNKNOWN_ERROR
                  MsgBox "Unknown error."
              Case Else
                  MsgBox "Error " & Err.Number & _
                  vbCrLf & Err.Description
          End Select
          Exit Sub

End Sub

Public Sub NewTape(pNewTape As String)

' Fill mTapeArray with tape symbols in pNewTape
Dim sTmp As String, x As Integer, Idx As Integer

mTapeStatus = "Unloaded"

pNewTape = pNewTape & ","
x = InStr(pNewTape, ",")
Idx = 0
Do While x > 0 And Idx < TapeLen
    Idx = Idx + 1
    sTmp = Trim$(Left$(pNewTape, x - 1))
    ' Check for valid symbol
    If mSymbols.IsSymbol(sTmp) Then
        mTapeArray(Idx) = sTmp
        pNewTape = Mid$(pNewTape, x + 1)
        x = InStr(pNewTape, ",")
    Else
        MsgBox "Invalid symbol in new tape: " & _
            sTmp, vbCritical
        Idx = 0    ' Want all blanks in this case
        Exit Do
    End If
Loop

' Fill remaining tape cells with blanks
For x = Idx + 1 To TapeLen
    mTapeArray(x) = Blank
Next x

mCurCell = 1
```

```
mCurState = mInitialState
mTapeStatus = "Loaded"

End Sub

Public Function SingleStep() As String

' Applies transition function
' Returns one of:
'    "NoMachine" if no machine
'    "NoTape" if no tape
'    "Inadmissible" if CurCell = 1 and Direction = L
'    "Undefined" if transition function not defined
'    "OffTheTape" if head moves past end of tape
'    "Admissible" otherwise

Dim RetValue As String
Dim pNewSt As String, pNewSym As String, pDir As
String

SingleStep = "Admissible"

' Check for machine and tape
If mMachineStatus <> "Loaded" Then
    SingleStep = "NoMachine"
    Exit Function
End If
If mTapeStatus <> "Loaded" Then
    SingleStep = "NoTape"
    Exit Function
End If

' Apply transition function
RetValue = mTransitions.Transition(mCurState, _
mTapeArray(mCurCell), pNewSt, pNewSym, pDir)

If RetValue = "Undefined" Then
    SingleStep = "Undefined"
Else
    ' Set new values
    mCurState = pNewSt
    mTapeArray(mCurCell) = pNewSym
    ' Move read/write head
```

```
        Select Case UCase$(Left$(pDir, 1))
            Case "R"
                ' Check for end of tape
                If mCurCell = TapeLen Then
                    SingleStep = "OffTheTape"
                Else
                    mCurCell = mCurCell + 1
                End If
            Case "L"
                If mCurCell = 1 Then
                    SingleStep = "Inadmissible"
                Else
                    mCurCell = mCurCell - 1
                End If
        End Select
    End If

End Function

Private Sub Class_Initialize()
mMachineStatus = "Unloaded"
mTapeStatus = "Unloaded"
End Sub
```

The User Interface

Figure 3.2 shows the user interface for the Turing machine project. The code behind this form is very straightforward — mostly just calls to *CMachine* class methods in the button click events.

```
' This is the visual interface

Dim CellWidth As Integer
Dim StepCt As Integer

Private CurMachine As CMachine

Private Sub cmdNewMachine_Click()

Dim MFile As String

' Get name of machine file and load it
```

```
MFile = InputBox("Enter name of machine file " & _
    "on directory containing Turing.exe.")

If MFile <> "" Then

    ' Get complete path and name
    MFile = App.Path & "\" & MFile

    CurMachine.ReadMachineFile MFile
    If CurMachine.MachineStatus = "Loaded" Then

        ' Update the form
        lblDesc = CurMachine.Description
        ShowTapeHead
        ListTransitions
        cmdNewTape.SetFocus
        StepCt = 0

    End If
End If

End Sub

Private Sub cmdNewTape_Click()

Dim sTape As String

' Get new tape and show it
sTape = InputBox$("Enter tape symbols, " & _
    "separated by commas. Max number of symbols " &_
    Str$(TapeLen))
If sTape = "" Then Exit Sub
txtNewTape.Text = sTape

' NewTape method to fill tape
CurMachine.NewTape sTape

ShowTapeHead
cmdSingleStep.SetFocus
StepCt = 0

End Sub
Private Sub cmdSingleStep_Click()
```

```
Dim RetValue As String

' Check for final state
If CurMachine.CurState = CurMachine.FinalState Then
    txtStatus.Text = "Final state"
    txtStatus.BackColor = vbYellow
    Exit Sub
Else
    RetValue = CurMachine.SingleStep
    StepCt = StepCt + 1

    ' Display results
    ShowTapeHead
    txtStepNumber.Text = StepCt
    txtStatus.Text = RetValue
    If txtStatus.Text = "Admissible" Then
        txtStatus.BackColor = vbWhite
    Else
        txtStatus.BackColor = vbRed
    End If
End If

End Sub

Private Sub cmdRun_Click()

' Repeat SingleStep_Click

Const MaxComps = 200
Dim SafetyCt As Integer

Do
    SafetyCt = SafetyCt + 1
    cmdSingleStep_Click
    Delay 0.5

Loop Until SafetyCt > MaxComps Or _
    txtStatus.Text <> "Admissible"

End Sub

Private Sub cmdExit_Click()
```

```
' Release object variable and unload form
' Break circular references first --
' not important here since we are terminating
' the program -- but good to keep in practice
If Not (CurMachine.Transitions Is Nothing) Then
    Set CurMachine.Transitions = Nothing
End If
If Not (CurMachine Is Nothing) Then
    Set CurMachine = Nothing
End If
Unload frmTuring
End Sub

Private Sub Form_Load()

Dim i As Integer

' Some positioning of controls for 1280x1024
CellWidth = TextWidth("eee")
txtTape(1).Width = CellWidth
txtTape(1).Height = TextHeight("E")
txtHead.Height = TextHeight("E")
txtHead.Left = txtTape(1).Left
txtHead.Width = TapeLen * CellWidth

' Load additional text boxes
For i = 2 To TapeLen
    Load txtTape(i)
    txtTape(i).Visible = True
    txtTape(i).Left = txtTape(i - 1).Left + _
      CellWidth
Next i

' Create new machine object
Set CurMachine = New CMachine

End Sub

Private Sub ShowTapeHead()

' Update the tape and head contents

Dim i As Integer
```

```
' Display tape contents
For i = 1 To TapeLen
    txtTape(i).Text = CurMachine.Tape(i)
Next i

' Change color of tape cells to move head
For i = 1 To TapeLen
    txtTape(i).BackColor = vbWhite
Next i
If CurMachine.CurCell > 0 Then
    txtTape(CurMachine.CurCell).BackColor = vbGreen
End If

' Show CurrentState in read/write head
' (in red if FinalState)
txtHead.Text = CurMachine.CurState
If CurMachine.CurState = CurMachine.FinalState Then
    txtHead.BackColor = vbRed
Else
    txtHead.BackColor = vbGreen
End If

End Sub

Private Sub ListTransitions()

' Fill the list box on the form with the
' transitions for snoopy users

Dim i As Integer, sTmp1 As String, sTmp2 As String

' Show list box
lstTrans.Clear

Dim objVar As CTransition
For i = 1 To CurMachine.Transitions.Count

    ' Faster to avoid repeated calls to Item method
    Set objVar = CurMachine.Transitions.Item(i)

    sTmp1 = objVar.CurSymbol
    If sTmp1 = " " Then sTmp1 = Blank
```

```
         sTmp2 = objVar.NewSymbol
         If sTmp2 = " " Then sTmp2 = Blank

         lstTrans.AddItem objVar.CurState & "," & _
            sTmp1 & "," & objVar.NewState & "," & _
            sTmp2 & "," & objVar.Direction

Next i

End Sub
Sub Delay(rTime As Single)

' Delay rTime seconds (min=.01, max=300)
Dim OldTime As Variant

' Safety net
If rTime < 0.01 Or rTime > 300 Then rTime = 1
OldTime = Timer
Do
     DoEvents
Loop Until Timer - OldTime >= rTime
End Sub
```

The Standard Module

To complete the project, we code the standard module with a few constant declarations and a call to the *Show* method of the main form.

```
' Copyright (C) 1996 by Steven Roman.
' All rights reserved.

Public Const Blank = "_"

' Enough for examples
Public Const TapeLen = 20
Public Const MaxSymbolsCt = 25
Public Const MaxStateCt = 25

' Run-time error constants
Public Const ERR_DUP_KEY = 457   ' VB's error number

' Logical error constants
```

```
Public Const ERR_BLANK_SYMBOL = vbObjectError + 1024
Public Const ERR_DUP_SYMBOL = vbObjectError + 1025
Public Const ERR_INVALID_SYMBOL = vbObjectError + _
   1026

Public Const ERR_BLANK_STATE = vbObjectError + 1124
Public Const ERR_DUP_STATE = vbObjectError + 1125
Public Const ERR_INVALID_STATE = vbObjectError + _
   1126

Public Const ERR_INVALID_DIR = vbObjectError + 1127

Public Const ERR_DUP_TRANS = vbObjectError + 1224

Public Const ERR_MACHINE_NOT_FOUND = vbObjectError _
   + 1224
Public Const ERR_NO_ALPHABET = vbObjectError + 1225
Public Const ERR_NO_STATES = vbObjectError + 1226
Public Const ERR_NO_TRANS = vbObjectError + 1227

Public Const ERR_NO_MACHINE_LOADED = vbObjectError _
   + 1324
Public Const ERR_NO_TAPE_LOADED = vbObjectError + _
   1325

Public Const ERR_INADMISSIBLE = vbObjectError + 1424
Public Const ERR_UNDEFINED = vbObjectError + 1425

Public Const ERR_UNKNOWN_ERROR = vbObjectError + _
   9999

Sub Main()
frmTuring.Show
End Sub
```

A Final Comment

We have implemented the Turing machines tape as a *Variant* property of the
CMachine class. We could have implemented the tape as a collection object as
well. For practice, you might wish to consider adapting the code in this way.

Just for fun, you may also try your hand at constructing new Turing machine files to do the following:

- Right-shift a binary string and park the head (thus losing the leftmost bit).
- Add two integers. An integer n is represented by placing n consecutive 1's on the tape. The summands are placed on the tape consecutively, with a single blank in between the two numbers. Thus, to start the computation of $3 + 4$, the initial tape appears as 111_1111. The output should be 1111111.

Chapter 4
OLE Automation Objects

What Is OLE Automation?

In this chapter, we discuss the remarkable world of *OLE automation*. The idea behind OLE automation is actually quite simple, and yet the technique has incredible power. Briefly put, OLE automation allows the programmer to make his or her classes (and hence their objects) available to other applications. In fact, the Enterprise Edition of Visual Basic allows classes to be made available across networks, which essentially means that objects can be made available to anyone in the world!

When an application makes some of its classes available to other applications, it is referred to as an *OLE automation server*. We will abbreviate this to *OLE server*, or just *server* (although there are other kinds of servers). An application that creates and uses objects from an OLE automation server is called an *OLE automation client* (or just *client*).

Visual Basic programmers can write both client and server applications. Also, many commercial applications can act as either clients or servers. For instance, Microsoft Excel version 7.0 makes public a total of 130 classes, which can be used in Visual Basic applications. On the other hand, Microsoft Word 7.0 offers only a single class, called *WordBasic*, but that class provides access to Word's powerful macro language.

The intent of OLE automation is that a client can treat a server's *public* class modules as if they were part of the client's own application. In particular, a client can declare an object variable of the server's class and instance that class, to create a new object. Such objects are referred to as *exposed objects*, because they are still part of the server, although they can be used by the client, just like the client's own objects.

OLE automation offers incredible potential, since it implies that the features of an OLE client application can potentially be *extended* by any OLE automation server in existence. Thus, if you need a certain feature that does not exist in a client application, there may be an existing server that provides this feature, or you can write one yourself!

In addition, OLE automation offers the virtue of *reusable* code, since a single server can service multiple clients at the same time. Moreover, since OLE server components are physically distinct from their clients, servers can be easily modified, for enhancement or error correction. If this modification does not affect the *existing* portion of the public interface, then client applications need not be changed.

Before proceeding, we should note that OLE, which, incidentally, no longer stands simply for *Object Linking and Embedding*, includes several other components besides OLE automation. For instance, one component of OLE is the use of an *OLE container control* for linking or embedding objects between applications. Another is the *OLE custom control*. We will focus attention strictly on OLE automation, however.

In one sense, making classes available to other applications is extremely easy. All we need to do is set the *Public* property of a class module to *True*, in which case we refer to the class itself as *public*. In fact, the only difference between an ordinary application and an OLE automation server is that the latter has at least one public class module!

Aside from the *Public* and *Name* properties, a class module has only one other property, called *Instancing*. This property is only in effect if the class is public; it has three possible values:

- *Creatable MultiUse*. This value means that a client can create as many objects as it wishes from the class.
- *Creatable SingleUse*. This value means that a client can create only one object from the class. Each additional request from the client for an object of that class is met by running an additional copy of the server.
- *Not Creatable*. This means that the client is not allowed to *create* any objects from the class, although a client can use objects that are created by the server in response to an *indirect* request from the client. (We will see an example of this later.)

Public Really Means Public

It is important to realize that *all* public variables and public methods in a public class are made available to other applications. There is no way to make a variable or procedure in a *public* class accessible to the rest of the application but *not* to other applications. It's all or nothing, so to speak.

On the other hand, a public variable declared in a *standard* module is public to the application but not *directly* accessible to other applications. For instance, if we declare a public variable

```
Public gTest aAs Integer
```

in a standard module in the server, then there is no direct way to refer to this variable from a client. Of course, the use of public variables to hold class data is, as you know, a violation of the rules of encapsulation, and thus not a good object-oriented technique. But it can have its place. For instance, we may want to implement a *read-only* property that uses a global variable to hold a server-wide value, such as the name of the server itself, as in

```
gSrvName=App.ProductName
```

The data in *gSrvName* are sometimes referred to as *static class data*.

To provide external access to the variable *gSrvName*, we define a public property within a public class that gets the value of *gSrvName*:

```
Public Property Get SrvName() As Integer
SrvName = gSrvName
End Property
```

Note that since the *SrvName* property is read-only, not much harm can be done. However, if the property were not read-only, we would be asking for big trouble, since several clients may be using the server at the same time, and thus one client could change the value while another client was using that value!

The Plan for This Chapter

Despite the simplicity of "going public," there are several issues that need to be addressed in order to produce a properly functioning OLE automation server. Here are a few of the major ones:

* Which objects in the server's object hierarchy should be exposed and how?
* Should the server have a visible interface?
* Should the server be an *in-process* server or an *out-of-process* server?

Before proceeding, let us discuss the organization of the rest of this chapter. First, we will consider how OLE automation clients and servers communicate with each other. This provides an insight into what is taking place underneath the surface — from the viewpoint of the OLE systems programmer — and will help us appreciate what Visual Basic must do in response to a few simple lines of code that we may write. More to the point, it will help us understand *why* we write these lines of code.

We then consider an example of how to create a simple OLE automation server and how to test it with a simple client. The steps are very straightforward and amount to little more than we have already done in previous chapters, but with some additional attention paid to issues such as giving the project a suitable name, for use by prospective clients.

Finally, we will discuss a series of issues that pertain to creating more substantial servers. These issues include

- How servers are started and ended
- Registering and unregistering servers in the system Registry
- Visible interface issues
- Handling errors
- Testing an OLE server
- Object hierarchies
- Issues specifically related to in-process servers
- Version compatibility issues

Communication Between OLE Automation Clients and Servers

OLE automation is, above all, a mechanism for sharing information, in the form of code and data. Thus, it requires communication between the server and the client, which is often complicated by the fact that the applications may not be running in the same address space or may not even be on the same computer.

At the surface, Visual Basic makes the communication seem effortless — as though the server's classes were actually part of the client's code. In fact, the simplicity of the code used to employ OLE automation in Visual Basic belies the complex and fascinating things that are taking place underneath the surface.

Our plan is to take a brief, and very simplified, glimpse at OLE communication, so we can better understand the issues facing us at the Visual Basic level. Thus, we will be delving into the realm of the OLE systems programmer. OLE systems programming is usually done, at the Windows programming level, using C or C++. However, Visual Basic programmers are quite capable of creating sophisticated clients and servers, without the need to implement some very complex programming strategies.

The Communication Problem

To get a feel for the problem of client/server communication, consider how communication takes place between a class module and other modules in the *same* application. Consider, for example, the class *CStudent*, defined below. We have made some changes in this class from the previous chapters, because we want the public interface to consist *entirely* of methods (as it should), with no public variables. (We also removed one exam, to shorten the code.)

```
Private mExam1 As Single
Private mExam2 As Single

Public Property Get Exam1() As Single
Exam1 = mExam1
End Property
Public Property Let Exam1(pExam1 As Single)
mExam1 = pExam1
End Property

Public Property Get Exam2() As Single
Exam2 = mExam2
End Property
Public Property Let Exam2(pExam2 As Single)
mExam2 = pExam2
End Property

Public Function Average() As Single
Average = (Exam1 + Exam2) / 2
End Function
```

Communication with the *CStudent* class module, from another module within the same application, for the purposes of creating and using an object of type *CStudent*, is done as follows:

```
Dim objStudent as CStudent
```

```
Set objStudent = New CStudent
Set objStudent.Exam1=75
Set objStudent.Exam2=55
MsgBox objStudent.Average
```

Of course, the compiler has no trouble understanding the type *CStudent*, since it is a user-defined type that is "defined" by inserting a new class module and giving it the name *CStudent*. Similarly, the compiler has no trouble identifying the properties *Exam1* and *Exam2*, because they are defined in the class module, which is part of the application. Finally, the compiler has no trouble calling the *Average* method, since it knows the method's address, along with its return type and parameter types, which are also defined in the class module.

On the other hand, if the class *CStudent* is in a separate (server) application from the client application that wishes to use it, then none of the previous code, *by itself*, will mean anything to the client. In fact, the first line will generate the error message *User-defined type not defined*. The last three lines would generate the error message *Method or data member not found* if indeed they could be reached by the compiler. Thus, we have a client/server communication gap.

Supplying Information to the Client

There are several approaches that the OLE server programmer can take to provide information to a prospective client. These approaches depend upon the form in which the server supplies information to the client. They include

1. an *IUnknown* interface
2. an *IDispatch* interface
3. a type library
4. a vtable interface

The performance quality of these methods can vary considerably, and the choice of which methods to implement is up to the programmer of the server. (The first method *must* be implemented by all OLE servers, however.)

We will explain each of these methods and show how they relate to Visual Basic programming. Note that Visual Basic implements all of the methods for us, but the code that we write may determine which interface is used in a given situation. Note also that, in order for an interface to be used, the server and the client must both support the interface.

What Is an Interface?

In general terms, an *interface* is just a set of related functions that provides a particular service. To provide an interface to a client, the OLE programmer (or, in our case, Visual Basic) simply includes a table that contains the addresses of the functions; that is, a table of *pointers* to the functions. Such a table is called a *virtual function table*, or *vtable* (abbreviated VTBL).

The Vtable Interface

Perhaps the most obvious way to provide information about the addresses of a public class's methods is simply to provide a vtable containing those addresses.

For instance, the four property methods *Property Let Exam1*, *Property Get Exam1*, *Property Let Exam2*, *Property Get Exam2* and the *Average* method can be made available to other applications through a vtable, as shown below, where *ptr* means *pointer to*. Thus, *ptrAverage* is the address of the *Average* method within the server.

vtable

ptrPropLetExam1
ptrPropGetExam1
ptrPropLetExam2
ptrPropGetExam2
ptrAverage
. . .

Note that a vtable contains only addresses. It does not contain the names, parameter information or return types of the functions in the interface. Thus, by itself, a vtable is of little use. Additional information on how to use the vtable is clearly needed. This information is provided in a so-called type library.

Type Libraries

A *type library*, also called an *object library*, is simply a file (or part of another file) that contains information about a server's public classes and their properties and methods.

In particular, a type library contains the names of the various public classes, the names of their properties and methods, and type information about parameters and return values, among other things. These libraries are used by *object browsers*, such as Visual Basic's Object Browser, to display object information to the programmer. A type library can be included as part of an application's executable file (EXE or DLL), or it can be a separate file, with extensions such as TLB or OLB.

OLE Interfaces

Information in a type library or a vtable is available to a client when the client is compiled. This is a big advantage, since the client can incorporate the information directly into its executable, which makes for much more efficient code. However, some servers do not supply type libraries or vtables, and some clients are not capable of taking advantage of them, even when they are supplied.

For this reason, OLE provides a different means of getting information, in the form of functions that can be called by the client to obtain the required information. Unfortunately, this method incurs a performance penalty, since additional code must be included in the client's executable, to make the requests, and extra run time is needed to receive the information.

The OLE functions that supply information to the client are grouped into special OLE interfaces. Two of these interfaces are particularly germaine to OLE automation — *IUnknown* and *IDispatch*. (The *I* stands for *interface*.)

The *IUnknown* Interface

All OLE automation servers *must* implement an interface called *IUnknown*, for each of its exposed objects. This simple interface is responsible for two things: It keeps the reference count for the object, and it provides information on which other interfaces are implemented for that object. (An OLE programmer can implement his own or her custom interfaces, as well as additional OLE interfaces.)

In particular, the *IUnknown* interface consists of three functions:

- *AddRef* increments the reference count for the object.
- *Release* decrements the reference count, freeing the object when the reference count falls to zero.
- *QueryInterface* supplies information on what other interfaces the object implements.

The vtable for the *IUnknown* interface of an object can be pictured as follows.

vtable

ptrAddRef
ptrRelease
ptrQueryInterface

Although keeping the reference counts and supplying information about additional interfaces is extremely important, the *IUnknown* interface does not supply much information about the object itself. For instance, it does not allow access to an object's properties or methods. The *IDispatch* interface is designed for this purpose.

The *IDispatch* Interface

The *IDispatch* interface provides a way for a client to access the properties and methods of an exposed object. This interface contains the following two functions (and more):

- *GetIDsOfNames* gets a special ID number, called the *Dispatch ID*, or DISPID, of a given property or method, from the name of that property or method. (The value of the DISPID for each property and method is determined by the OLE programmer.)
- *Invoke* calls a method or gets or sets a property, using the DISPID.

Any parameters that are needed to call a particular method are sent as parameters to the *Invoke* function. The syntax of the *Invoke* function has the following form:

```
Invoke(<Dispatch ID number of method or property>,
   <reserved>,
   <language related (i.e., English, French)>,
   <method, property get or property let?>
   <pointer to an array with the parameters to pass>,
   <pointer to a place for the return value>,
   <don't worry about it>,
   <error info>)
```

The *Invoke* function is like a *wrapper* for an object's methods and properties. When a client calls *Invoke*, this function processes any parameters, accesses the property or calls the method identified by DISPID, and then passes any values back to the client, through the return parameter.

A vtable that implements the *IUnknown* and *IDispatch* interfaces has the following appearance.

vtable

ptrAddRef
ptrRelease
ptrQueryInterface
ptrGetIDsOfNames
ptrInvoke
. . .

Binding

Before we see how Visual Basic uses these various interfaces, we must briefly introduce the concept of binding. In the theory of programming languages, the term *binding* refers to forming an association between two entities. For instance, the line

```
Dim x As Integer
```

binds the variable name *x* to the type *Integer*.

When a particular binding takes place at compile time, it is called *static binding*, or *early binding*. When binding takes place at run time, it is called *dynamic binding*, or *late binding*. Static binding provides a major performance advantage over dynamic binding, since code to do the binding does not have to be included in the run-time executable, resulting in smaller and faster-running executables. Thus, in general, static binding is to be preferred over dynamic binding.

Putting It All Together

As we have mentioned, the server programmer can choose which interfaces he or she wishes to implement, with the exception that the *IDispatch* interface must be implemented. This leads to several possibilities, which we now explore.

Using a Vtable — Early Binding

The most efficient form of client/server communication comes when the server implements a vtable interface, along with a type library, and the client understands how to use these items.

In this case, the client can get information about property and method names, argument types and return types from the type library, and it can get actual addresses from the vtable. Moreover — and this is the key point — the client can get all of this information at *compile time*, so the information can be incorporated *directly* into the client's executable code. This is early binding.

In fact, Microsoft refers to this approach in its documentation as *very early binding*, but there is a bit of confusion in terminology, since Microsoft also refers to this method, in its Knowledge Base, simply as *early binding*, or as *vtable binding*. The latter term is the most descriptive, and so we will use it here.

In any case, vtable binding is the method of choice. Unfortunately, not all servers or clients support the vtable approach, although all clients and servers created using Visual Basic do. When vtable binding is supported by the server, we may code a Visual Basic client using the same code we would use if the server's public classes were contained in the client application, which is precisely the goal of OLE automation. Thus, the code

```
Dim objStudent as CStudent
Set objStudent = New CStudent
Set objStudent.Exam1=75
Set objStudent.Exam2=55
MsgBox objStudent.Average
```

will make perfect sense to the client, even though the *CStudent* class may be in another part of the world!

Of course, in order to take advantage of a type library, a Visual Basic client application needs to know that the library exists. The existence and location of the type library are provided to the client by setting a reference to the type library in the *References* dialog box, shown in Figure 4.1. Notice that the type library file name is given, for the highlighted reference, near the bottom of the dialog box.

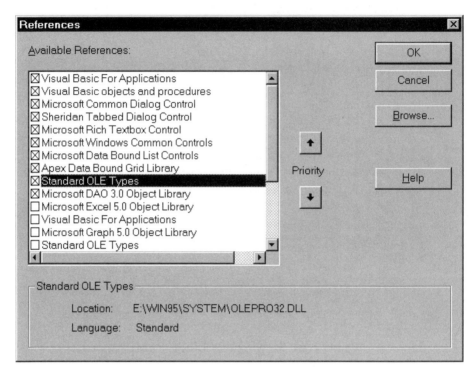

Figure 4.1

Using a Type Library, but No Vtable — ID Binding

If a server supplies a type library but no vtable, or if the client understands type libraries but not vtables, then all is not lost. The client can use the type library to get all the information it needs *except* for the actual addresses of the methods.

Thus, the client can incorporate a great deal of information about the server at compile time. In addition to the class name, property and method names, parameters types and return types, the type library also contains the DISPIDs of the class's methods, which can therefore also be bound at compile time. As a result, to call a method, the client need only call the *Invoke* function of the *IDispatch* interface. It does not need to call *GetIDsOfNames*.

Thus, a server can implement the *IDispatch* interface, along with a type library. Clients that use these two services can perform early binding of names, types and DISPIDs but must call *Invoke*, which performs late binding of method names to the actual method code. Microsoft refers to this approach as *early binding* in its documentation, and more properly as *ID binding*, in its Knowledge Base.

No Type Library — Late Binding

If a server does not provide a type library, or if the client does not know how to use a type library, then the client has no way of getting object information at compile time. Thus, for instance, code such as

```
Dim objStudent as CStudent
Set objStudent = New CStudent
```

will not be understood by the client compiler. In this case, the client must resort solely to the *IDispatch* interface, using both *Invoke* and *GetIDsOfNames*. Unfortunately, calls to these interface functions can place a considerable performance hit on the communication process.

But if the client has no prior knowledge of the server's classes, how can it even ask for an object? The answer is that Visual Basic supplies the client programmer with a generic object variable declaration and a generic object creation request that does not trigger any *type unknown* errors from the compiler. (We have encountered generic object variable declarations before.) In effect, the client can say to the server "I have a generic object variable. Please fill it with an object from your class named . . . ." Of course, the client programmer gets the names of the server's public classes from the server's *documentation*!

The following code (in the client) will successfully declare an object variable named *objStudent*, create an object of type *CStudent* and set *objStudent* to refer to that object. (The server's application name is *StudentServer*.)

```
Dim objStudent As Object
Set objStudent = _
  CreateObject("StudentServer.CStudent")
```

Once the object has been created, its properties and methods can be called as before.

```
Set objStudent.Exam1=75
Set objStudent.Exam2=55
MsgBox objStudent.Average
```

Note that the generic syntax *As Object*, in the first line above, avoids the type name *CStudent*, of which the *compiler* knows nothing. This is the proper use of the *As Object* syntax.

In order for the client to implement generic object creation, it must use the fully qualified class name *StudentServer.CStudent* to request an object of that class, and then somehow get a pointer to the object's *IDispatch* interface so it can call the object's methods. This is where the Windows Registry comes in. To understand how, we need to look at class IDs.

Class IDs

Every public class in an OLE server must have a unique identifier so that it can be differentiated from all other public classes in the world (remember that OLE automation can take place over networks). OLE takes the interesting approach of assigning to each public class a number called a *Class ID*, or CLSID. In an effort to make it very unlikely that any two class IDs anywhere on the earth will ever be the same, OLE uses a 128-bit number, called a *globally unique identifier* (GUID) or *universally unique identifier* (UUID). This number is pseudorandomly generated by the OLE programmer (or, in our case, by Visual Basic) using a special utility called GUIDGEN.EXE, which simply produces a new GUID and copies it to the clipboard for use by the programmer.

As an aside, let us see if we can get a grasp on just how unlikely it is that two randomly generated 128-bit numbers are identical. (Although there is no such thing as a perfect random number generator, we will assume so for the sake of this discussion.) A measurement shows that an ordinary deck of 52 playing cards is 5/8-inch thick and an astronomy book reveals that the nearest star, *Proxima Centauri*, is 4.3 light-years from the Earth. Since a light-year is about 5.9×10^{12} miles, a straightforward calculation shows that a stack of 2^{128} playing cards has height 1.1×10^{19} light years, which would reach about 2.6 *billion billion* times the distance to *Proxima Centauri*. Enough said.

Since CLSIDs are just a bit too unwieldy for humans to use, OLE also recognizes a public class by its *fully qualified class name*, also called the *Programmatic ID*, or *ProgID*. This string consists of the class name, qualified by the server's name, as in *StudentServer.CStudent*. While there is a much greater chance that this name will not be unique, it will still be quite unlikely, provided that the programmer chooses reasonably sized names. (There are about 4×10^{22}, or 2^{75}, possible programmatic IDs whose class and server names are each 8 characters long.)

The Registry

When a server is installed on a computer, it must be registered in the system Registry. This is done automatically upon installation by any server application whose setup program was created by the Visual Basic Setup Wizard. We will discuss registering and unregistering a server later. Figure 4.2 gives a peek at the Registry contents for *StudentServer*. (This information has been gleaned from various locations within the Registry. It is not all together as you see it here.)

To help identify when two GUIDs are equal, we have marked them with small figures. The numbers marked with a triangle are the GUID for the type library itself, and the numbers marked with a circle are the Class ID for the public class *CStudent*.

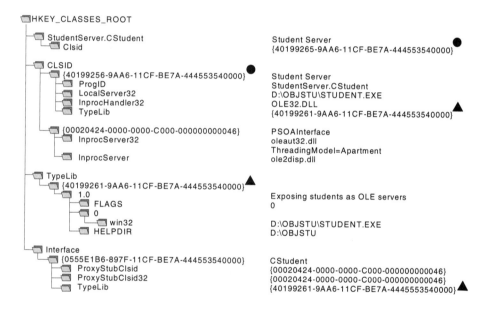

Figure 4.2

There are four branches to the Registry entries for the *StudentServer* project. The first branch provides a means to obtain the CLSID from the programmatic ID, or put another way, to obtain the number of the class from its name. The second branch supplies information about the *CStudent* class from the CLSID. In particular, it gives the ProgID, the name and location of the executable file and the type library's GUID. The third branch gives information about the type library, including the name of the library file (in this case, the server itself). Note the type library version number (1.0), which we will discuss when we talk about version compatibility. The final branch contains a GUID for the *CStudent* class's *interface*, that is, its set of properties and methods. We will also discuss this when we talk about version compatibility.

Now, the client application can use the programmatic ID, which appears in the *CreateObject* code line

```
Set objStudent = _
   CreateObject("StudentServer.CStudent")
```

to look up the Class ID for *CStudent*. This, in turn, can be used to get the file name and location of the server, which can be started if it is not already running.

At this point, the client (or, in our case, Visual Basic) can call a special Windows OLE function called *CoCreateObject*, which creates the requested object and returns a pointer to the object's *IUnknown* interface. The client can then use *QueryInterface* to get a pointer to the *IDispatch* interface, and then call *GetIDsOfNames* and *Invoke* to execute each of the following lines:

```
Set objStudent.Exam1=75
Set objStudent.Exam2=55
MsgBox objStudent.Average
```

Since binding of *objStudent* to the *CStudent* type, as well as binding of the names *Exam1*, *Exam2* and *Average* to the actual methods of the same name, does not take place until run time, all binding under this scenario is *late binding*; hence, Microsoft's choice of name for this approach. Perhaps *IDispatch binding* would be a better name, albeit less meaningful to Visual Basic programmers who may not have read this book!

It is worth repeating that, while Visual Basic does support vtable binding, we may wish to write a Visual Basic client that uses a server that does not support either vtables or type libraries. In such a case, we *must* use generic object declarations and creation requests.

In-Process and Out-of-Process Servers

We have mentioned that a client and its server may be running in the same address space or in different address spaces. Let us explore this point further.

This is not the place to go into details about address spaces, so we will be brief.

In the 32-bit world of Windows 95 and Windows NT, a running application is referred to as a *process*. Windows gives each process a separate 2 GB *virtual address space*. The term *virtual* means that the addresses are not actually those of physical memory — very few of us are lucky enough to have 2 GB of RAM chips! But the process doesn't care about whether or not there is actual memory behind its addresses, for it is the job of the Windows *virtual memory manager* to map virtual memory addresses to physical memory addresses (or to disk if necessary) when code that uses these addresses is running.

Simply put, each process gets to use address numbers from, say for the sake of argument, 0 to 2 GB. Thus, for example, when code in one process refers to virtual address &H00111111, it can *only* mean address &H00111111 in that process's own address space. It is thus impossible for one process to refer (directly) to another process's addresses.

The use of separate address spaces is designed to provide protection of one process from other processes. On the other hand, the *process boundary* makes *desired* communication between processes much more complicated. Since OLE automation depends on communication between the client and the server, if these applications run in separate address spaces, OLE must step in to deliberately break down the address space boundary.

When creating a 32-bit OLE server in Visual Basic, the programmer must decide whether to create an *in-process* server that will run in the same address space as the client that requests its services or to create an *out-of-process* server that will run in a separate address space. In-process servers are DLL files, whereas out-of-process servers are EXE files. (Visual Basic will not create a 16-bit in-process server.)

The choice depends on the desired goals. An in-process server is frequently the better choice from the point of view of performance, or if the server needs to provide a visual interface, such as a dialog box to request information from the client. On the other hand, an out-of-process server is needed if a single server is to service multiple clients, or if the server is also designed to be run as a stand-alone application, as in the case of Microsoft Excel, for instance.

We will have much more to say about the differences between in-process and out-of-process servers later in the chapter. Let us conclude this discussion here with a word about out-of-process communication.

Marshalling — The Proxy-Stub Connection

When out-of-process communication is necessary, OLE makes it *appear to the client* that communication is taking place within the client's own address space, thus relieving the client of the task of making what is termed a *remote process call*, or RPC.

As shown in Figure 4.3, this is done by setting up a "dummy" object, called a *proxy object*, in the client's address space. The client interacts with the ersatz object, thinking it is the genuine article. When the client makes a call to a function in one of the object's interfaces, it makes the call to an address in the proxy object. The proxy object, in turn, prepares the data and makes a remote process call to the *object stub* in the server's address space. The object stub calls the real function, gets the return information (if any) and shuffles it back to the object proxy, for delivery to the client. The process is referred to as *marshalling*.

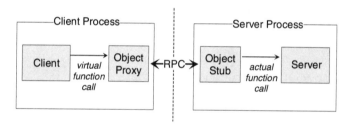

Figure 4.3

Creating a Simple OLE Automation Server

Now that we have a general overview of some of the issues involved in OLE client/server communication, we can return to the level of the Visual Basic programmer. Perhaps the best way to proceed is to go through the steps required to create a very simple server and a corresponding client. As always, we suggest you key in and save the following project, for future tinkering.

Creating a Simple Server

The modest purpose of our server, known as *StudentServer*, is to expose the *CStudent* class, so that a client can create a *CStudent* object, set the *Exam1*,

Exam2, and *Exam3* properties and then invoke the *Average* method. Thus, our server does not need a visual interface.

We begin by starting a new project and removing the default *Form1* file from the project, since we don't want a visible interface. To create a startup procedure, we insert a (standard) module into the project and give it the name *basStudent*. Then we add a *Sub Main* procedure to *basStudent*. The procedure needs no code, since the server need do no initialization.

Preparing the Public Class

Now we insert the *CStudent* class and set its properties to

- Public: *True*
- Name: *CStudent*
- Instancing: *Creatable MultiUse*

As mentioned, the latter means that a client can create as many *CStudent* objects as desired. Next, we place the following code in the *CStudent* class module.

Snippet 4.1 — StudentServer

```
'' (In CStudent class module)
Public Exam1 As Single
Public Exam2 As Single
Public Exam3 As Single

Public Function Average() As Single
Average = (Exam1 + Exam2 + Exam3) / 3
End Function
```

Setting the Project Options

Finally, we need to set the project options. Figure 4.4 shows the project dialog box for *StudentServer*.

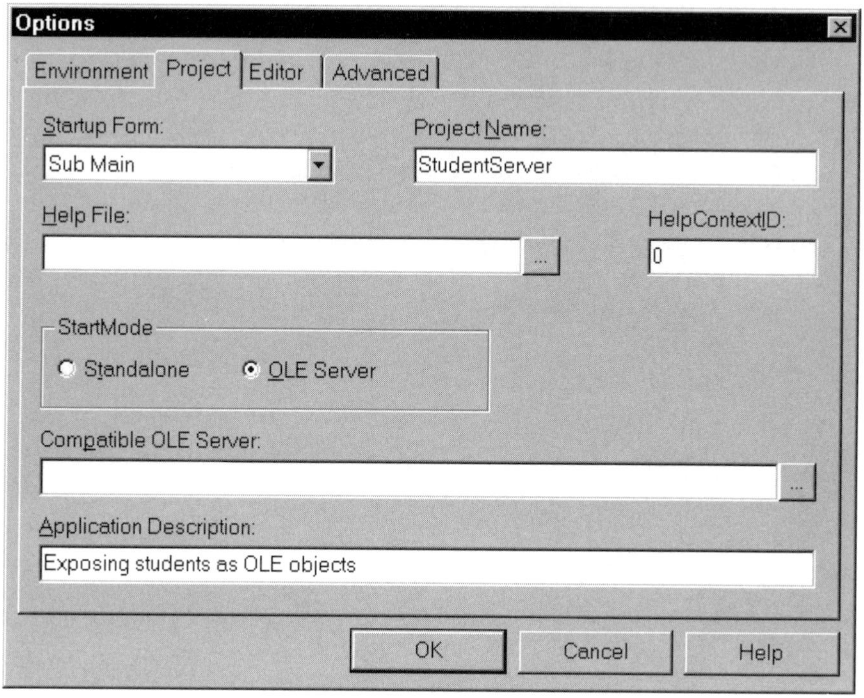

Figure 4.4

In the *Startup Form* drop-down box, we check that *Sub Main* is showing, as it should be because we removed the default form. Since our server has no visual interface, we do not want a form popping up when the server is started, which is why we removed the form. However, even if a visual interface is desired, it is generally a good idea to set the *Startup Form* option to *Sub Main*, so that we may place any initialization code in that procedure before displaying a form.

The next step is to choose a project name. Since this name forms the first part of the programmatic ID of any exposed classes, the name should be informative, not too short, and hopefully unique (at least to our machine)! We choose *StudentServer*.

The *StartMode* frame contains two option buttons. For reasons we will discuss very soon, if an OLE server is started under the Visual Basic IDE, then Visual Basic will immediately determine that the server is not being used and terminate it! Thus, for testing purposes, the *StartMode* option should be set to *OLE Server*, which will keep the server running, so that we can get a client going and request an object or two, to keep the server alive. Note that this feature has no bearing on an EXE or DLL server file — it is strictly for testing the server under Visual Basic.

Incidentally, there is also a read-only property called *StartMode*. This property can be tested in the startup code for the server to reveal how the server was started. To wit, if *StartMode* equals 0, the server was started as a stand-alone application (possible only with an EXE file). If *StartMode* equals 1, then the server was started by OLE, in response to a request. By setting the *StartMode* option in the *Project* dialog box, the programmer can test any corresponding startup code in *Sub Main*.

We will postpone a discussion of the *Compatible OLE Server* option until later. The *Application Description* text box just gets a short phrase describing the application. This is the help text string that appears in Visual Basic's Object Browser when the *StudentServer* type library is selected. Incidentally, to create a help description for the public class *CStudent*, open the Visual Basic Object Browser, choose the *CStudent* class and hit the *Options* button. Then type "Student Server" in the Description text box and click OK.

That's it. Save the project and run the server from within the Visual Basic IDE. You should always use the Ctrl-F5 key to run the server, so that the entire project is compiled at startup. This will catch any compile-time errors now, before the server is used. If the server terminates immediately, recheck the *StartMode* option in the Project window.

A Small Client and the Three Forms of Binding

Now let's create a simple client and use it to communicate with the server. We will refer to this project as *StudentClient* and will have occasion to use it again as well. To get a clear field, minimize the running server project. Then start a new copy of Visual Basic. We suggest you save the following project as well, since we will be experimenting with it from time to time.

Let us first try late binding. At this point, the client does not know about the server's type library, since we have not referenced it in Visual Basic's *References* dialog box. In the *Form_Load* procedure, place the following code.

Snippet 4.2 — StudentClient

```
Private Sub Form_Load()

Dim i As Integer, OldTime As Variant

Dim objStudent As Object
Set objStudent = _
  CreateObject("StudentServer.CStudent")

OldTime = Timer

' A loop to check performance
' Shorten this loop for a non-Pentium
For i = 1 To 500
  objStudent.Exam1 = 50
  objStudent.Exam2 = 70
  objStudent.Exam3 = 80
Next i

MsgBox "Average: " & objStudent.Average & _
  "   Time: " & Timer - OldTime

End Sub
```

Running the client should produce a message box displaying the average 66.66666. On a Pentium 90, the time for this computation is about 11 seconds.

You might also try adding an extra line of code to this event as follows:

```
objStudent.Exam8 = 50
```

This code will still compile correctly, even though the *Exam8* property does not exist! The point here is that late binding implies that this error will not be caught until the client attempts to *access* the property.

To try ID binding, we need to tell the client about the server's type library. Choose the *References* menu item from the *Tools* menu. Search the list box for *Exposing Students as OLE objects* and check its box. Now the client can access the type library. Start the Object Browser (F2) and choose the library *StudentServer*. You should see one public class (*CStudent*) with three properties (*Exam1*, *Exam2* and *Exam3*) and one method (*Average*). If not, then double-check that you have started the server and that *CStudent* is public. Now run the client. You should get the same average as before. The time to completion is about 10 seconds on a Pentium 90 computer.

Finally, to try vtable binding, change the first two lines of code in the *Form_Load* event to

```
Dim objStudent as CStudent
Set objStudent = New CStudent
```

As an experiment, remove the reference to the server in the References dialog box and then run the code. As expected, you should get the error message *User-defined type not defined*. Now, reestablish the reference and run the client. You should get the usual average. The time to completion on a Pentium 90 computer has dropped to around four seconds!

Referencing the Server's Type Library

We have seen that in order for a client to use a server that employs early or ID binding, the client must hold a reference to the server's type library. This is done in the *References* dialog box in the client's Visual Basic IDE.

When testing a server running under Visual Basic, with a client that is also running under Visual Basic, you may find that you are starting and stopping both programs frequently. Under these conditions, some care must be taken to ensure that the client always has a valid reference to the server's type library.

Problems arise because the client uses the running server's type library GUID as its reference to the server. However, each time the server is restarted, Visual Basic computes a new GUID for it, thus breaking the previous reference. After a server restart, the client's *References* dialog box will show the line

MISSING: *Exposing Students as OLE objects*

Moreover, each time the server is restarted, it gets a new GUID. Thus, terminating and restarting the server when the client is running will leave the client holding an invalid GUID. This will lead to the error message *OLE automation error* when the client tries to use the type library.

One way to handle this is to make it a rule to start (or restart) the client each time you restart the server. Another approach is to create a preliminary EXE (or DLL) file for the server. Visual Basic places a GUID for the type library in this file. If we put the name of this file in the *Compatible OLE Server* text box in the *Project* dialog box, Visual Basic will use this GUID number when the server is started from within Visual Basic. In fact, Visual Basic will reference the EXE or DLL when the server is not running under Visual Basic, and it will reference the VBP project file when the server is running under Visual Basic.

If changes to your server make it incompatible with the preliminary EXE version, you will need to make a new EXE file and refresh the reference to it in the client. We will discuss the issue of version compatibility later in this chapter.

Another item worth mentioning in this connection is that, while the client holds a reference to the server, you will not be able to make a new EXE file in the server project. To do so, you must remove the reference in the client.

Registering and Unregistering a Server

There are several approaches to registering or unregistering a server.

Registration During Installation

As mentioned earlier, if the server is being installed on a customer's system, it will be registered automatically during setup if the setup program was created using the Visual Basic Setup Wizard.

Manual Registration Outside the Visual Basic IDE

To register or unregister a server manually from outside the Visual Basic development environment, the following choices are available:

- An out-of-process (EXE) server is registered when it is run for the first time.
- An out-of-process (EXE) server can be registered, without running any of its code, by running the server with the switch */regserver*, as in *student.exe /regserver*. It can also be unregistered using the */unregserver* switch, as in *student.exe /unregserver*. Of course, this can be done using the *Run* option on the Start Menu under Windows 95 or the *File Run* option under the Windows NT Program Manager.
- An in-process (DLL) server (which cannot be executed like an EXE file) can be registered using a special program called *regsvr32.exe*, which is located on the Visual Basic CD-ROM. The syntax is *regsvr32 [/u][/s]*

dllname, where /*u* is used for unregistering and /*s* is for silent running (no success/failure message).

- An OLE server (EXE or DLL) can also be registered by selecting it using the Browse button from the *References* dialog box of the Visual Basic IDE.

Manual Registration Inside the Visual Basic IDE

Finally, an OLE server is temporarily registered whenever it is run from within the Visual Basic IDE and is permanently registered whenever it is made into an executable (EXE or DLL).

How Servers Are Started and Ended

It is not necessary to explicitly start an OLE server (by clicking on an icon, for instance). In fact, it is not even possible to do so with an in-process server, since it is a DLL. OLE automation servers are started whenever a client makes a request of the server.

As we have seen, when the reference count of an object reaches zero, Visual Basic destroys that object. In a similar vein, Visual Basic will automatically terminate a running server if all of the following conditions hold:

- No code in the server is running or is waiting in the calls list to be run.
- The server is not in the process of being started by a client request.
- For an in-process server, there are no references to any of the server's objects (and hence all objects have been destroyed). For an out-of-process server, there are no *external* references to any of the server's objects.
- For an out-of-process server, there are no *loaded* forms. For an in-process server, there are no *visible* forms. (*Hidden* forms do not stop an *in-process* server from terminating.)

It is important to remember that if we want a server to terminate *grace-fully*, we should let Visual Basic terminate the server in the natural course of events. There is no need to manipulate events to keep a server alive or close it unnaturally.

This applies especially to the *End* statement, since it causes an *abrupt* termination of the server, without allowing *Terminate* events to fire. It also implies that we should not implement any form of the *Quit* command for a client to use to terminate a server, since there may be more than one client using the server at the same time!

Indeed, the proper procedure is simply to release references and unload forms when they are not needed, and let Visual Basic take care of terminating the server.

The first condition listed above for server termination simply says that a server will not be terminated if it has code running or waiting to be run. The latter applies to the case where the server has called a procedure in another server, has called a function in a DLL or has made an API function call, for instance.

The second condition is needed in order to deal with a matter of procedure involving OLE, and it need not concern the programmer. In particular, there is a slight delay between the initial request (by OLE) to open a server and the point at which the reference is actually made to the object that caused the request. During this period, no objects are references and the server might otherwise close.

The last two conditions require a bit more discussion and we will devote complete sections to each of them.

Reference Counts for Servers

For an out-of-process server, Visual Basic keeps a separate reference count for *external* references to the server's objects; that is, references from outside the server itself. It is only these external reference counts that keep an out-of-process server from terminating. For an in-process server, there is only one reference count. Let us put this to the test.

Make the following inclusions to the *CStudent* class module in the *Student-Server* project. The purpose of these inclusions is to create an internal circular reference within the server.

Snippet 4.3 — Additions to StudentServer

```
' New object property
Public Deskmate As CStudent

Private Sub Class_Initialize()
Beeps 2
End Sub
```

```
Private Sub Class_Terminate()
Beeps 3
End Sub
```

Add the following code to the standard module *basStudent* in the server:

```
'' (In the standard module basStudent)
' Global variables
Dim objStu1 As New CStudent
Dim objStu2 As New CStudent

Sub Main()

Beeps 5

' Circular reference
Set objStu1.Deskmate = objStu2
Set objStu2.Deskmate = objStu1
End Sub

Sub Beeps(iCount As Integer)
Dim OldTime As Variant, i As Integer
' Delay 1 sec
OldTime = Timer
Do: Loop Until Timer - OldTime >= 1.5

' iCount beeps of speaker, 0.5 secs apart
For i = 1 To iCount
OldTime = Timer
Do: Loop Until Timer - OldTime >= 0.5
Beep
Next i

End Sub
```

Note that we have added code to cause the speaker to beep twice whenever the *Initialize* event is fired, thrice whenever the *Terminate* event is fired and five times when the *Sub Main* procedure is executed, which happens only when the server is started. Using beep counts is a useful trick to determine when things happen in a server, since it does not involve the complications of using visual messages or saving information to a disk file. As we will discuss later, a simple message box will not work, since it may not be accessible underneath another application's windows. Now, save the project and create an out-of-process server (EXE file) named *Student.exe*.

Next, make the following changes in the client project. First, remove all the code from the *Form_Load* event. Then add command buttons called *Start* and *Exit* to the form. Add the following code to the *Click* button events.

Snippet 4.4 — Additions to StudentClient

```
Private Sub cmdExit_Click()
Unload Me
End Sub

Private Sub cmdStart_Click()
Dim i As Integer, OldTime As Variant

' Late or ID binding
Dim objStudent As Object
Set objStudent = _
  CreateObject("StudentServer.CStudent")

objStudent.Exam1 = 50
objStudent.Exam2 = 70
objStudent.Exam3 = 80

objStudent.Average

MsgBox "Average: " & objStudent.Average

Set objStudent = Nothing

End Sub
```

Save the project and create an executable file called *Client.exe*. Run this executable and listen for beeps. Here is what you should see and hear:

1. Five beeps, indicating that the server is starting.
2. Two beeps, indicating that *objStu1* is being initialized.
3. Two beeps, indicating that *objStu2* is being initialized.
4. Two beeps, indicating that *objStudent* is being initialized.

5. A message box with the student's average (dismiss the box).
6. Three beeps, indicating that *objStudent* is being terminated.
7. Three beeps, indicating that *objStu1* is being terminated.
8. Three beeps, indicating that *objStu2* is being terminated.

After step 6 above, there are no longer any *external* references to the server, and although the server still has internal object references (a circular reference, in fact), Visual Basic terminates the server. As a result, you will hear two more sets of three beeps as the internally referenced objects are destroyed. Moreover, if you hit the *Start* button again, you will hear a set of five beeps, indicating that the server is being *restarted*.

Now try the same experiment with an in-process server. Terminate the running client and switch to the Visual Basic server application. To distinguish between the DLL you are about to make and the EXE that you have already made, go to the *Sub Main* event and change the line

```
Beeps 5
```

to

```
Beeps 8
```

Now make a DLL file using the *Make OLE DLL File* option under the *File Menu*.

Start the client EXE file. Here is what you should see and hear:

1. Eight beeps, indicating that the in-process server is starting.
2. Two beeps, indicating that *objStu1* is being initialized.
3. Two beeps, indicating that *objStu2* is being initialized.
4. Two beeps, indicating that *objStudent* is being initialized.
5. A message box with the student's average (dismiss the box).
6. Three beeps, indicating that *objStudent* is being terminated.

At this point, the client and server are both running, even though the client holds no references to any of the server's objects. You can verify this by hitting the *Start* button again. You should hear just two beeps, indicating that the *objStudent* object is being created. You will not hear the eight beeps from *Sub Main*, precisely because the server is still running.

Incidentally, a look at the system Registry will reveal that both the EXE and the DLL versions of the server are registered. By changing the beep count from five to eight for the *Sub Main* procedure, we were able to discover that when both servers are registered, the in-process DLL gets priority.

As a final experiment, close the client application and switch to the server again. Comment out the two lines

```
Set objStu1.Deskmate = objStu2
Set objStu2.Deskmate = objStu1
```

in the *Sub Main* procedure of the server, so that the server will hold no internal object references. Now save the application and create a new DLL. Start the client. You should see and hear the following:

1. Eight beeps, indicating that the in-process server is starting.
2. Two beeps, indicating that *objStudent* is being initialized.
3. A message box with the student's average (dismiss the box).
4. Three beeps, indicating that *objStudent* is being terminated.

At this point, the client is still running but the server has terminated. To verify this, hit the *Start* button again. You will hear eight beeps, indicating that the server is *restarting*.

Since we are temporarily done with the two servers (EXE and DLL), you may wish to test your unregistering skills. To unregister the EXE version, run the server with the syntax

student.exe /unregserver

To unregister the DLL, run the *regsvr32.exe* program, with syntax

regsvr32.exe /u Student.dll

Servers with a Visual Interface

We have already mentioned that an out-of-process server will not terminate if it has any loaded forms, be they visible or not. There are several reasons why a server may include forms.

Servers with Dialog Boxes

One reason that a server may contain forms is that it may want to present a dialog box to the user, to convey information or to request input. In the latter case, if the input is completely of the client's making, it may be better to let the client pass the input as a parameter to a method, or as the value of a property. But if the server needs to present a list of options to the client, for instance, then a dialog box is appropriate.

However, in the case of an out-of-process server, there are serious difficulties involved in displaying server forms while the client is the active application. As the Visual Basic documentation puts it,

> Because there is no natural relationship governing focus and modality between forms exposed by two different applications — that is, by an out-of-process OLE server and a client application — this functionality is best implemented with an in-process OLE server.

Simply put, we cannot rely upon the user of the client application to be able to detect the presence of a form that is displayed by the server, for it may be completely hidden underneath the client's windows or the windows of other running applications. Hence, when a server requires a visual interface *only* to provide communication with the client, and is not intended to be a stand-alone application, it should probably be implemented as an in-process server.

For an in-process server, dialog boxes do not present too many difficulties. Since the client and the server are running in one process space, there is only one active window and only one window has the keyboard focus. There are two things to keep in mind, however. First, Visual Basic does not allow *modeless* forms in an in-process server. Attempts to include such a form will generate a run-time error. Second, error messages should *not* be displayed by the server. We will discuss the issue of how to handle errors from an OLE server later in the chapter.

OLE Servers That Also Function as Stand-Alone Applications

Another reason for including forms in a server is that the server may also function as a stand-alone application. Put another way, a stand-alone application may also expose objects to other applications. This is certainly the case with Microsoft Excel, for instance.

To clarify the issues, we should think of the user of the stand-alone application as a special type of client. Let us refer to this type of client as a *stand-alone client*, to differentiate it from an OLE client. Thus, it may happen that a particular server has a stand-alone client using its visual interface, along with one or more OLE clients using exposed objects, as shown in Figure 4.5.

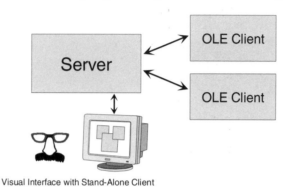

Visual Interface with Stand-Alone Client

Figure 4.5

In any situation where more than one client is using a given server, care must be taken to ensure that no client do anything to disrupt another client's use of the server. In particular, no client should be allowed to summarily shut down the server.

Thus, the server should *not* provide a *quit method* that allows an OLE client to shut the server. Nor should the server provide a *quit command* available through a menu choice or command button, for this would allow a stand-alone client to shut down the server.

On the other hand, OLE clients are given the opportunity to "clean up" after themselves by releasing all object references, and stand-alone clients must be accorded the same privilege. Accordingly, the server must provide a "quit" command that gives the *appearance* of shutting down the server, by closing all files that the stand-alone client has opened and unloading all forms that the stand-alone client has opened. This allows the server to close when all other clients have cleaned up after themselves.

In simple terms, for instance, the *File Exit* command in a stand-alone/server application could actually say, "Clean up my mess, and shut down only if no other clients are using you."

Handling Errors

Handling errors in an OLE server is not difficult, provided that we remember one important principle: *Never let a server display an error message. Either handle the error without a message or pass the error to the client.*

Passing error information to the client is no different than passing error information up the calling tree within a single application. In fact, for the purposes of error handling, the calling procedure in the *client* sits atop the server's calling tree!

Figure 4.6 depicts a typical situation. A client procedure calls a method in a server. The method then calls a procedure within the server. An error occurs in that procedure. Under these circumstances, if the error goes untrapped or is reraised in an active error handler, it will proceed up the calling tree — first to the method in the server and then to the calling procedure *in the client*.

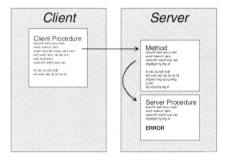

Figure 4.6

This feature makes error handling in a client/server situation essentially the same as it is within a single application, with the one exception that error messages should not be presented until we reach the client.

To be more specific, we have seen that error information can be passed to a calling procedure as the return value of a function or as the value of a parameter to the function. This applies equally well to errors in server methods. Alternately, we may pass errors by not trapping the error or by raising a fresh error in an active error-handler, until the error reaches the calling procedure in the client.

Note that when raising an error from within the server, for passing to the client, we must remember to use error numbers in the range

$$vbObjectError + 512 \ \text{to} \ vbObjectError + 65535$$

Also, it is important to return a description of the error in *Err.Description*.

To illustrate these points, and a few others, try the following. In the *CStudent* class module, add one method and one private subroutine as follows. The intention of the latter is to generate an error, so if you have an x drive, make an appropriate change in that line.

```
Public Sub TestError()
Call AnError
End Sub

Private Sub AnError()
Open "x:\test" For Input As #1
End Sub
```

Next, in the *StudentClient* project, comment out or delete the existing lines in *cmdStart_Click* and replace them with the following code:

```
Private Sub cmdStart_Click()

On Error GoTo ErrClient

Dim objStudent As Object
Set objStudent = _
  CreateObject("StudentServer.CStudent")
objStudent.TestError

Set objStudent = Nothing

Exit Sub

ErrClient:
Stop
Exit Sub
End Sub
```

Before running this project, check the *Advanced* tab on the *Options* dialog box, to make sure the *Break on Unhandled Errors* option is selected. Now set a breakpoint in *StudentServer* on the line *Call AnError* and start the server. Then switch to the client, start it and hit the *Start* button. Trace through the server from the breakpoint. When you run the line that causes the error, you should be taken immediately back to the *client's* error-handler. If instead you get an error message, recheck the *Break on Unhandled Errors* option.

Not only does this little experiment show that unhandled errors are sent to the client, but it also demonstrates two additional points. First, you can set breakpoints and trace through servers while a client is running. Second, to test error handling, the correct error-breaking option must be chosen in the *Advanced* dialog box under the *Options* menu. It is easy to forget to do this and consequently spend considerable time trying to figure out why things are not working as expected!

Be Nice

As the Visual Basic documentation points out, there are some design issues to be considered when returning errors to the client. These issues are really no different than the issues involved in error passing within a single application, but their importance is magnified, since the client programmer is often not the person who programmed the server. In short, the programmer of the server should be mindful of the client programmer's point of view. Above all, the programmer should supply careful and complete documentation with regard to the behavior of the server in *all* aspects, not just in the matter of how errors are returned.

Errors from Your Server's Servers

When we write an OLE server that calls another OLE server, we must deal with errors from the second server. As with internal errors, these errors should be either handled within our server, without generating error messages, or passed to the client.

In the latter case, it is important to remember that our clients are not going to be happy if we say, in effect, "A server that I am using has generated an error. Too bad." Indeed, it is our responsibility to present the error to the client as though it came from our server, which, from the client's point of view, it did! Accordingly, if our server does not handle the error internally, then we should reraise the error with *our server's own* error number, error description and error source parameters. If there is some information about the second server that we wish to pass on to our client, then it should be done from within our own error description.

In short, we are responsible to the clients of our server, and so our server should not pass the buck to another server!

One final note: Any errors that may occur during OLE's cross-process communication between a client and an out-of-process server will be raised in the client and not in the server. Thus, we may need to deal with such errors as well.

Externally Creatable and Dependent Objects — The Object Hierarchy

We have discussed the concept of an object hierarchy in Chapter 1, where it was pointed out that an object hierarchy is designed to express the notion of *containment*. A small hierarchy for the *StudentServer* project is shown below.

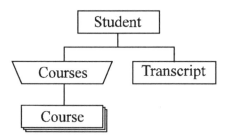

The *Courses* class is a collection class that contains the individual courses a student is taking.

In implementing this object hierarchy, we first observe that there is no reason why a client should be allowed to create a *Transcript* object or a *Courses* collection object *independently* of a *Student* object, since the former objects cannot exist without a student to which they belong.

In fact, a client should be allowed to create objects of type *Transcript* or *Courses* only as a property of a previously created *Student* object. After all, this is the intended meaning of the object hierarchy. In short, a client should not be allowed to ask the server for a *Transcript* object, but it should be allowed to *use* the *Transcript* property of a *Student* object.

This is easily accomplished through implicit creation, using the *New* keyword. This permits the creation of an object by making a *reference* to that object. Thus, for instance, if we declare a property of type *Transcript* in the *Student* module as follows:

```
Public Transcript As New CTranscript
```

then a client can simply *refer* to this property of an existing *Student* object. Visual Basic will take care of the creation of a *Transcript* object for the property.

Furthermore, in order to prevent a client from directly instancing the *Transcript* class, we set the class properties of *CTranscript* to

- Public: *True*
- Instancing: *Not Creatable*

The public setting is required in order for a client to refer to the *Transcript* property, and the *Not Creatable* setting prevents a client from *directly* instancing the class. Thus, the *only* way a client can create a *Transcript* object is by reference to the *Transcript* property of an existing *Student* object.

Incidentally, an alternative to using the *New* keyword would be to make the declaration

```
Public Transcript as CTranscript
```

and then place the following code in the *Initialize* event of the *CStudent* class:

```
Set Transcript = New CTranscript
```

The downside of this approach is that a *Transcript* object is created as soon as the client creates a *Student* object, even if the client never needs the *Transcript* object.

Of course, we also want to set the properties of the *Courses* and *Course* classes to *Public*, *Not Creatable*. In this way, objects of these classes can be created only indirectly. In the case of the *Course* class, objects will be created using the *Add* method of the *Courses* object.

Any *public* class that has its *Instancing* property set to *Creatable MultiUse* (or *SingleUse*) is said to be an *externally creatable class*, and its objects are *externally creatable objects*. Thus, the *Student* class is externally creatable. A *public* class whose objects are contained in another class, and whose *Instancing* property is set to *Not creatable*, is called a *dependent class*, and its objects are *dependent objects*. Thus, the *Transcript*, *Courses* and *Course* classes are dependent.

Let us take a look at the code to implement our *Student* object-hierarchy.

Snippet 4.5 — The Student Object-Hierarchy

The *CStudent* class should contain the code

```
Public Exam1 As Single
Public Exam2 As Single
Public Exam3 As Single

' Object properties declared with New keyword
Public Transcript As New CTranscript
Public CourseLoad As New CCourses

Public Function Average() As Single
Average = (Exam1 + Exam2 + Exam3) / 3
End Function
```

The *CTranscript* class module gets only two properties:

```
Public Level As String
Public Units As Integer
```

The *CCourse* class module gets two properties as well:

```
Public CourseName As String
Public CourseProf As String
```

The *CCourses* collection class gets the usual *Count* property, along with the *Item* and *Add* methods.

```
Private mCourses As New Collection

Public Property Get Count() As Long
Count = mCourses.Count
End Property

Public Function Item(vKey As Variant) As CCourse
Set Item = mCourses.Item(vKey)
End Function

Public Function Add(CourseName As String, _
  CourseProf As String) As CCourse
```

```
Dim objCourse As New CCourse
With objCourse
    ' Set properties
    .CourseName = CourseName
    .CourseProf = CourseProf
    ' Add to collection
    mCourses.Add objCourse
End With
' Return object
Set Add = objCourse
End Function
```

Finally, the standard module *basStudent* just needs an empty startup procedure *Sub Main*:

```
Sub Main()
End Sub
```

Now we turn to the client, which consists of a single form, containing an *Exit* button and a *Start* button. Here is the code.

Snippet 4.6 — The Client

```
Private Sub cmdExit_Click()
Unload Me
End Sub

Private Sub cmdStart_Click()

Dim objStudent As Object
Dim objLoad As Object

' Create student
Set objStudent = _
  CreateObject("StudentServer.CStudent")

' Implicitly create transcript object property
objStudent.Transcript.Level = "Senior"
```

```
' Set object variable for convenience
Set objLoad = objStudent.CourseLoad

' Add to collection
objLoad.Add "Music 1A", "W. Mozart"

' Display results
MsgBox "Course: " & objLoad.Item(1).CourseName & _
    vbCrLf & "Prof: " & objLoad.Item(1).CourseProf

' Not needed, but just a habit
Set objStudent = Nothing
Set objLoad = Nothing

End Sub
```

It might be worth mentioning an issue of performance at this point. Notice that we declared and set an object variable as follows:

```
Set objLoad = objStudent.CourseLoad
```

even though it was not strictly necessary to do so. We did this for performance reasons (although in this simple example it really doesn't matter). To wit, the code

```
objStudent.CourseLoad
```

requires a call to the server's *CourseLoad* property method. This may require an out-of-process call, which can be slow. By using the *objLoad* variable, we limit this to a single call, which can save considerable time in a large project. The moral is to use object variables to store the values of properties, thus avoiding repeated calls to the same property method.

In-Process Issues

There are certain restrictions to keep in mind when creating an in-process server. Here is a partial list. Some of the following items have been mentioned previously, and a more complete list is available in the Visual Basic *Professional Features* documentation.

- In-process servers are 32-bit only.
- In-process servers cannot use the *Creatable SingleUse* property of a public module.
- The *End* statement is not allowed in an in-process server.
- In-process servers cannot use modeless forms. Since a startup form is always modeless, no startup forms are allowed in an in-process server.
- A visible modal form will prevent an in-process server from terminating, but a *hidden* modal form will not.
- The *Sub Main* startup procedure in an in-process server is intended to be used for initialization code only. It should therefore be as short as possible and should not display any forms or message boxes. It should not use the *DoEvents* function.
- In general, the *DoEvents* function should be used very cautiously in an in-process server, since it may allow code in the client — such as code in a timer event — to execute. If, for instance, the code in the timer event releases the reference to the object whose method contains the *DoEvents* function, an error will result.
- Unlike an out-of-process server, internal circular references will keep an in-process server running, even after all *external* references have been removed. Also, public variables defined in a standard module in the server, that hold references to the server's objects, will prevent the server from terminating.
- When the client of a *running* in-process server terminates, the *Terminate* events of the server's *internally* created objects are not executed.
- If a fatal error occurs in an out-of-process server, the server will terminate, but the client may still run, although any references to the server's object that the client holds will dangle. However, a fatal error in an in-process server will also terminate the client!

We should also say a few words about testing an in-process server. When an in-process server is tested within the Visual Basic development environment, the server is running in the address space of the Visual Basic environment. The client is also running in its own address space or in that of another instance of Visual Basic. Hence, it is not possible to test an in-process server and its client in the same address space. The best we can do is set the *Use OLE DLL Restrictions* option in the *Advanced* dialog box of the *Options* menu for the server. This will instruct Visual Basic to apply the same restrictions as would be normally applied if the server were running as an in-process server. For instance, an error message will appear if we include an *End* statement in the code, and we will be informed, if necessary, that a DLL must use a *Sub Main* as its entry point.

Version Compatibility

The issue of version compatibility can be a bit confusing at first, but it is really based on two straightforward actions on the part of Visual Basic, and all we need to do is be aware of the consequences of these actions. Before discussing this, however, let us consider what we might do to a server to change its compatibility.

How Compatibility Can Be Affected

There are three types of changes that we can make to a server to affect its compatibility; that is, the ability of *existing* clients to use the new server. Let us illustrate these changes with our usual example: the *CStudent* class module.

```
' The CStudent class module
Public Exam1 As Single
Public Exam2 As Single
Public Exam3 As Single

Public Function Average() As Single
Average = (Exam1 + Exam2 + Exam3) / 3
End Function
```

We will use the term *interface* to refer to the *public* attributes of the properties and methods of a class; that is, to the names, data types, number and types of parameters and return types of the properties and methods.

Version-Identical Servers

If changes to the server do not affect the interfaces of any public class modules, then the new server is said to be *version-identical* with the original server. For instance, changing the *Average* method to

```
Public Function Average() As Single
```

```
Average = 0.25*Exam1 + 0.25*Exam2 + 0.50*Exam3
End Function
```

does not affect the interface and so the new server is version-identical with its predecessor. Note, however, that while the return *type* and number of parameters for the *Average* method have not changed, the return *value* has changed. Thus, version-identical does not necessarily imply that the same input will produce the same output, as would happen if we made a version-identical performance enhancement to an existing method, for instance.

Version-Compatible Servers

If new properties or methods are added to a server's interface but changes are not made to any *existing* portion of the interface, then old clients can still use the original features of the new server, whereas new clients can use the new features as well. In this case, the new server is said to be *version-compatible* with the original server.

For instance, if we add a new property to the *CStudent* class

```
Public DeskMate as CStudent
```

the new server will be version-compatible with its predecessor.

Version-Incompatible Servers

If the public interface of a server is changed in such a way that old clients can no longer use the new server, then the new server is *version-incompatible* with the original server. This can happen under any of the following conditions:

- The project name is changed.
- The name of any *public* class module is changed.
- A *public* class module, variable, procedure or property is removed or is changed to *private*.
- The data type of a *public* variable, procedure or property is changed.
- The names, data types or order of appearance of the parameters of any *public* procedure or property in a *public* class are changed.

If any of these changes must be made, the new server should be thought of as a brand new application, for it will be treated as such by customers (clients). Indeed, in order for existing clients to retain access to the *original* server, the project name (and thus the programmatic ID) and the executable file name must be changed for the new server.

In fact, Visual Basic does everything it can to persuade us to create a new application when we make version-incompatible changes. In particular, it issues the following warning when the new server is saved as a Visual Basic project. (This message is the result of removing the *Average* method and saving the project.)

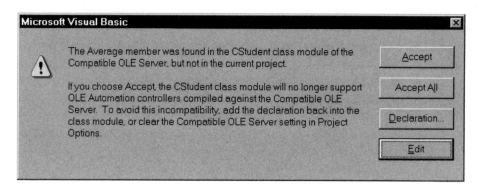

If we choose *Accept* and attempt to make an executable file, we will get the following message.

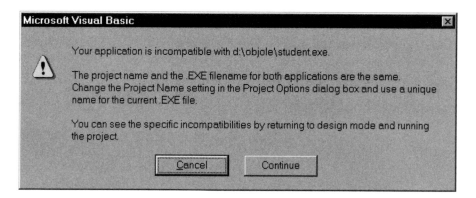

How Visual Basic Handles Compatibility

Now we can consider how Visual Basic handles each of the three types of compatibility. To judge compatibility, Visual Basic uses the server whose name we place in the *Compatible OLE Server* text box in the *Project* dialog box, for comparison with the new server. Let us refer to the server named in the *OLE Compatible Server* text box as the *reference server*.

Whenever we make a new EXE or DLL file, Visual Basic compares the interfaces of each public class with the interfaces of the reference server. Changes in compatibility are then recorded at two levels — through *type library version numbers* (at the type library level) and through *interface* GUIDs (at the individual interface level).

Type Library Version Numbers

To reflect compatibility with the reference server, Visual Basic records a *type library version number* in the server's executable file and in the system Registry. Incidentally, the type library version number is unrelated to the *file* version number of the executable, which we set under the *Make EXE* file dialog box.

You can see the type library version number, as recorded in the system Registry for the *CStudent* class, in Figure 4.2, which we repeat here for convenience (the version is 1.0).

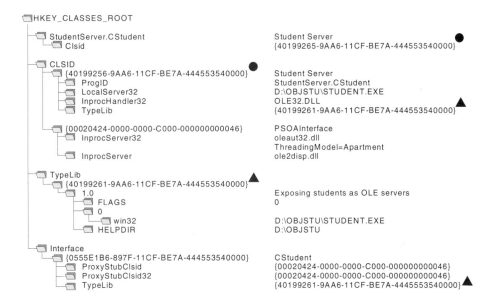

Figure 4.7

If the new server is version-identical with the reference server, then the type library version number is not changed for the new server. If the new server is version-compatible with the reference server, the minor type library version number is incremented in the new server, say from 1.0 to 1.1.

Interface GUIDs

Type library version numbers keep track of the general compatibility of a new server. If a new server is version-compatible with the reference server, then clients of the old server will, in *theory*, be able to use the new server.

In practice, a client recognizes an interface through the interface's GUID, which is kept in the server and also in the Registry, as shown in Figure 4.7. However, a new interface will get its own GUID. Thus, in order to maintain backward compatibility, the server (and the Registry) must keep copies of the GUIDs for *both* the new and the old interfaces.

Put another way, for a version-compatible change, Visual Basic will generate new GUIDs and place them in the executable (when it is created) and in the Registry (at server registration time) but will *not* remove the old GUIDs. This allows older clients to continue to use the original interface, but in the new version-compatible server.

Thus, in our example, if we were to add the *DeskMate* property to the *CStudent* class, Visual Basic would *add* the new interface to the server and generate a new interface branch of the Registry, as shown in Figure 4.8. Note that the *only* difference between this branch and the other *CStudent* interface branch is a new interface GUID. The type library GUID has not changed, for instance, because both interfaces use the same type library.

```
Interface
  {0555E1F0-897F-11CF-BE7A-444553540000}    CStudent
    ProxyStubClsid                          {00020424-0000-0000-C000-000000000046}
    ProxyStubClsid32                        {00020424-0000-0000-C000-000000000046}
    TypeLib                                 {40199261-9AA6-11CF-BE7A-4445553540000}
```

Figure 4.8

If we insist upon not taking Microsoft's advice and creating an incompatible server with the same project and executable names, the major type library version number will be changed, say from 1.0 to 2.0. Also, the old interfaces will be removed from the Registry. If the project name is the same but the executable name is changed, then *both* type library versions (and interfaces) will be listed in the Registry, but the programmatic ID can be bound only to one

CLSID, which smacks of trouble ahead. It is best simply to heed Microsoft's advice, and consider the version-incompatible server as a new application, with a new project name (hence a new programmatic ID) and a new executable name.

The Reference Server and Interim Builds

Now we come to the two potentially troublesome practices involved in version compatibility. Recall that when a new server is version-compatible with its reference server, Visual Basic increments the type library version number in the new server and registers the new interfaces in the Registry, without removing the old entries.

To illustrate the first potential problem, suppose that a server, with path *d:\objstu\student.exe*, has type library version number 1.0 and that this file is designated as the OLE Compatible Server for the project. If we make a version-compatible change, the new server would then have version number 1.1 and contain references to interface GUIDs for both versions. Also, the Registry will reference both interfaces.

But if the new executable has the same name and location as the previous executable, then it will overwrite the old file and automatically become the new OLE compatible server! Hence, if the next build is also version-compatible, it will become version 1.2 and will now contain *three* interface GUIDs — those from versions 1.0, 1.1 and 1.2. Also, the Registry will reference all three interfaces.

You can probably see where this is headed. By using the same executable file name (and path) for each new build of the server, we automatically change the OLE-compatible server, thus cluttering up the executable file with intermediate interface GUIDs and cluttering up the Registry (ours and the client's) with interfaces that are not used.

There are two solutions to this problem, both of which have some downsides. You can create an initial executable of a slightly different name, such as *student0.exe*, and declare it to be the OLE-compatible server. In this way, all interim builds will be compared to a "constant" server and will not accumulate interim interfaces. The downside is that version compatibility will *not* be checked between consecutive builds, leaving open the possibility that version 1.11 will not be compatible with version 1.10 and yet still be compatible with the initial version.

An alternative solution is to use a different name for the interim builds and then return to the original name *student.exe* for the final shipping version. This solution avoids the previous problem but will clutter up *your* system Registry with interim interfaces! Thus, the choice boils down to either doing your own checking for version incompatibility during interim stages (if you care, that is) or messing up your own Registry.

The second potential problem comes when we deliberately use different OLE-compatible servers at different stages in a project. For instance, suppose we have created a chain of version-compatible servers, each one using the *previous* one as a reference server, as follows:

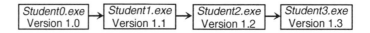

If we now changed (deliberately or accidentally) the OLE-compatible server reference to *Student0.exe* and created a new server, called *Student4.exe*, from the code used to create *Student3.exe*, Visual Basic would compare the new server to *Student0.exe* and give the new server the version number 1.1, as shown below.

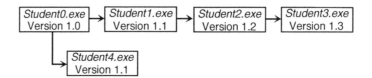

Thus, the new server would be an enhancement to version 1.3 and yet have version number 1.1! No good. This problem could also arise even if we didn't change the EXE names, if somehow the original EXE file overwrote the latest version.

Of course, these problems are easily avoided, simply by thinking through the process that Visual Basic uses to keep track of version compatibility.

Index